Go Big
KNITS

20 Projects Sizes 38 to 54

TRAFALGAR SQUARE
North Pomfret, Vermont

GoBig
KNITS

20 Projects Sizes 38 to 54

First published in the United States of America
in 2016 by
Trafalgar Square Books
North Pomfret, Vermont 05053

Originally published in French as *Tricot XXL*

ISBN: 978-1-57076-771-5

Library of Congress Control Number: 2016937050

Editorial director: Thierry Lamarre
Design and instructions: Charlotte Rion
Photography: Pierre Nicou
Backgrounds: Fotolia/Juri Samsonov
Concept: Bergère de France
Styling: Clémence Caurette
Hair and make-up: Isabelle Kryla
Retouching/digital editor: Jean Michel Boillot
Graphic design, interior layout @: Either Studio
Cover: Either Studio
Corrections/technical editing: Isabelle Misery and Véronique Blanc
Coordination at Bergère de France: Sofia Rivière and Josette Keller
Translation: Elizabeth Gray

Printed in China
10 9 8 7 6 5 4 3 2 1

SIZE EQUIVALENTS
S = 36, M = 38/40, L = 42/44, XL = 46/48, XXL = 50/54

Contents

Cléa

Raphaëlle

Patterns followed by an asterisk (*) are easier to make.

Cléa

Soft materials and patterns designed to show beautiful curves to their best advantage... Must-haves that are never out of style, for all seasons!

1
Ample cardigan

Worked in stockinette and k1, p1 ribbing,
using Plume and Métalika.

1. Ample cardigan

SIZES	S/M, 36 to 46	L/XL, 48 to 54
	Number of skeins	
PLUME, Light gray	13	16
MÉTALIKA, Galaxy	1	1
from BERGÈRE de France; Plume, CYCA #4 (worsted/afghan/ aran); 11% wool, 42% acrylic, 47% polyamide; 87 yd/80 m / 50 g), Métalika, CYCA #0 (thread; 38% polyamide, 62% metal-effect polyester; 711 yd/650 m / 25 g)		
Needles: U.S. sizes 8 and 9 / 5 and 5.5 mm		

Stitches used

K1, P1 RIBBING, with 1 strand PLUME and 1 strand MÉTALIKA held together, with both needle sizes. When working with yarns held together, make sure the sparkling effect of the MÉTALIKA is consistently visible.
Row 1 (RS): K1, p1 across.
Row 2: Knit into knit and purl into purl as sts face you.
Repeat Rows 1-2.

STOCKINETTE (St st), with PLUME, using larger needles.
Row 1 (RS): Knit.
Row 2: Purl.
Repeat Rows 1-2.

Gauge

It's very important to knit a gauge swatch (see "The Indispensable Gauge," page 86).
15 sts and 20 rows in stockinette on larger needles = 4 x 4 in / 10 x 10 cm.
Adjust needle sizes to obtain correct gauge if necessary.

Instructions

BACK
With smaller ndls and both yarns held together, CO 163 (169) sts.

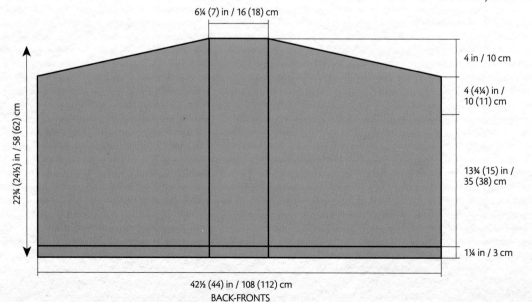

6¼ (7) in / 16 (18) cm

4 in / 10 cm

4 (4¼) in / 10 (11) cm

13¾ (15) in / 35 (38) cm

1¼ in / 3 cm

22¾ (24½) in / 58 (62) cm

42½ (44) in / 108 (112) cm
BACK-FRONTS

Work 1¼ in/3 cm / 8 rows in k1, p1 ribbing.
With larger needles and using only PLUME, continue in St st for 18¾ (20½) in/48 (52) cm / 98 (106) rows total.

Shape Shoulders:
S/M: BO 6 sts each at beg of next 2 rows, 7 sts each at beg of next 18 rows.
L/XL: BO 7 sts each at beg of next 18 rows, 8 sts each at beg of next 2 rows.
On next row, BO the rem 25 (27) sts for the neck.

LEFT FRONT

With smaller ndls and both yarns held together, CO 69 (71) sts.
Work 1¼ in/3 cm / 8 rows in k1, p1 ribbing.
With larger ndls and using only PLUME, continue in St st for 18¾ (20½) in/48 (52) cm / 98 (106) rows total.

Shape Shoulder:
S/M: BO 6 sts each at beg of next RS row, 7 sts each at beg of next 9 RS rows.
L/XL: BO 7 sts each at beg of next 9 RS rows, 8 sts each at beg of next RS row.

RIGHT FRONT

With smaller ndls and both yarns held together, CO 69 (71) sts.
Work 1¼ in/3 cm / 8 rows in k1, p1 ribbing.
With larger ndls and using only PLUME, continue in St st for 18¾ (20½) in/48 (52) cm / 99 (107) rows total.

Shape Shoulder:
S/M: BO 6 sts at beg of WS row, 7 sts each at beg of next 9 WS rows.
L/XL: BO 7 sts each at beg of next 9 WS rows, 8 sts at beg of next WS row.

SLEEVE CUFFS (make 2 alike)

With larger needles and both yarns held together, CO 41 (45) sts.
Work in k1, p1 ribbing for 8¾ (9½) in/22 (24) cm / 48 (52) rows, BO, and then set aside.

FRONT BANDS AND BACK NECK (make 2 alike)

With smaller needles and both yarns held together, CO 9 sts. Work in k1, p1 ribbing for 26 (28) in/66 (71) cm / 134 (144) rows and then BO all sts.

Finishing

Join shoulders.
Match center of each sleeve cuff to shoulder seam and pin cuff to shoulder with 4 (4¼) in / 10 (11) cm on each side of shoulder seam; sew pieces together. Seam the sides of the body.
Pin front bands to edge of each front and around neck to meet at center back. Seam bands to front edges and then seam bands at center back.

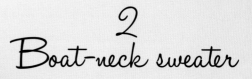

2
Boat-neck sweater

Worked in garter stitch, using Sonora.

2. Boat-neck sweater

Easy

SIZES	S	M	L	XL	XXL
	Number of skeins				
SONORA Night	5	5	6	6	7
from BERGÈRE de France; CYCA #3 (DK/light worsted; 50% cotton, 50% acrylic; 126 yd/115 m / 50 g)					
Needles: U.S. size 10½ / 7 mm					

Stitch used

GARTER STITCH: Knit all rows.

Gauge

It's very important to knit a gauge swatch (see "The Indispensable Gauge," page 86).

13 sts and 16 rows in garter stitch = 4 x 4 in / 10 x 10 cm.

Adjust needle size to obtain correct gauge if necessary.

Instructions

BACK

CO 52 (57, 62, 69, 76) sts. Work in garter stitch.

Armhole shaping: After working 12¼ (12½, 12½, 13, 13½) in/31 (32, 32, 33, 34) cm / 50 (52, 52, 54, 56) rows, on *each* side 2 sts in from edge:

S: Inc 1 st every 4 rows 4 times, 1 st every other row twice = 64 sts.

M and L: Inc 1 st every 4 rows 6 times = 69 (74) sts.

XL and XXL: Inc 1 st every 4 rows 4 times, 1 st every 6 rows twice = 81 (88) sts.

Now continue in garter st until approx. 5½ (6, 6¼, 6¾, 7) in/14 (15, 16, 17, 18) cm / 72 (76, 78, 82, 86) rows total from beg of armhole,

Shoulders and neck: Dec 2 sts on *each* side, 2 sts in from edge, on every other row:

(To dec 2 sts, 2 sts in from edge: K2, k3tog, k across until 5 sts rem, k3tog, k2.)

S and M: 7 times.

L, XL, and XXL: 8 times.

Knit 1 row across the remaining 36 (41, 42, 49, 56) sts and then BO.

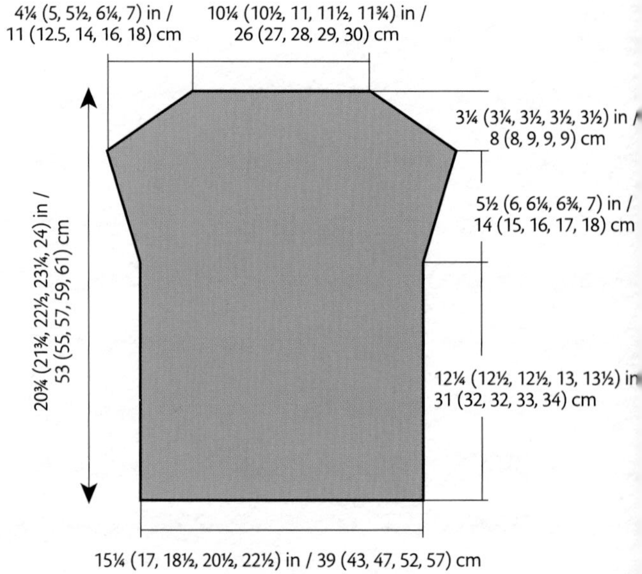
4¼ (5, 5½, 6¼, 7) in / 11 (12.5, 14, 16, 18) cm
10¼ (10½, 11, 11½, 11¾) in / 26 (27, 28, 29, 30) cm
3¼ (3¼, 3½, 3½, 3½) in / 8 (8, 9, 9, 9) cm
5½ (6, 6¼, 6¾, 7) in / 14 (15, 16, 17, 18) cm
12¼ (12½, 12½, 13, 13½) in / 31 (32, 32, 33, 34) cm
20¾ (21¾, 22½, 23¼, 24) in / 53 (55, 57, 59, 61) cm
15¼ (17, 18½, 20½, 22½) in / 39 (43, 47, 52, 57) cm

BACK-FRONT

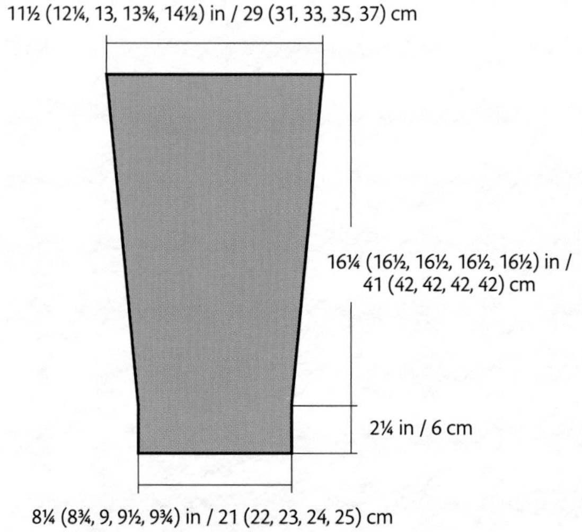
11½ (12¼, 13, 13¾, 14½) in / 29 (31, 33, 35, 37) cm
16¼ (16½, 16½, 16½, 16½) in / 41 (42, 42, 42, 42) cm
2¼ in / 6 cm
8¼ (8¾, 9, 9½, 9¾) in / 21 (22, 23, 24, 25) cm

SLEEVE

FRONT

Work as for back.

SLEEVES (make 2 alike)

CO 29 (30, 31, 32, 34) sts. Work in garter stitch.

After 2¼ in/6 cm / 10 rows, shape sleeve: on *each* side, 2 sts in from edge:

S: Inc 1 st every 12 rows twice and then 1 st every 14 rows 3 times = 39 sts.

M: Inc 1 st every 10 rows twice and then 1 st every 12 rows 4 times = 42 sts.

L: Inc 1 st every 8 rows 3 times and then 1 st every 10 rows 4 times = 45 sts.

XL and XXL: Inc 1 st every 8 rows 6 times and then 1 st every 10 rows twice = 48 (50) sts.

Continue in garter st until sleeve length is 18½ (18¾, 18¾, 18¾, 18¾) in/47 (48, 48, 48, 48) cm / 76 (78, 78, 78, 78) rows total; BO loosely.

Finishing

Join shoulders, leaving 34 (35, 36, 37, 38) sts free at center for neck. Attach sleeves to armholes and sew sleeves and side seams of sweater.

3
Tunic sweater

Worked in garter stitch, stockinette, and k1, p1 ribbing, using Galaxie.

3. Tunic sweater

SIZES	S	M	L	XL
	Number of skeins			
GALAXIE Sirius	13	14	15	17
from BERGÈRE de France; CYCA #6 (super bulky/roving; 2% polyester, 18% wool, 80% acrylic; 77 yd/70 m / 100 g)				
Needles: U.S. size 11 / 8 mm; 1 tapestry needle (for seaming and weaving in ends); some pins				

Stitches used

GARTER STITCH: Knit all rows.

STOCKINETTE (St st):
Row 1 (RS): Knit.
Row 2: Purl.
Repeat Rows 1-2.

K1, P1 RIBBING: Worked across an odd number of stitches.
Row 1 (RS): K1, p1 across.
Row 2: Work sts as they appear.
Repeat Rows 1-2.

Gauge

It's very important to knit a gauge swatch (see "The Indispensable Gauge," page 86).
11 sts and 13 rows in St st = 4 x 4 in / 10 x 10 cm.
Adjust needle size to obtain correct gauge if necessary.

Instructions

BACK
CO 48 (53, 58, 63) sts.
Set up pattern: 3 garter sts, 42 (47, 52, 57) sts in St st, 3 garter sts.
Work in pattern for 12¼ (12½, 12½, 13) in/31 (32, 32, 33) cm / 40 (42, 42, 44) rows,
Mark the armholes: On next row, tie a piece of scrap yarn or pm at first and last stitch for the beg of the armholes.

Continue in garter stitch and St st as before.

When piece measures 25¼ (26, 26¾, 27½) in/64 (66, 68, 70) cm / 84 (86, 88, 92) rows total, work 4 rows in garter stitch only.
Shoulders and neck: On next row, BO all sts (see page 27) and cut yarn, leaving a tail approx. 9¾ in / 25 cm long. This strand can be used in seaming during finishing.

FRONT
Work as for back.

LOWER EDGE BAND
CO 13 sts. Work in k1, p1 ribbing for 32¼ (35½, 38½, 42½) in/82 (90, 98, 108) cm / 106 (118, 128, 140) rows.
BO all sts and cut yarn, leaving a tail approx. 4 in / 10 cm long.

Finishing

Seam the shoulders with an invisible seam (see "Tips," page 87) about 3¼ (4, 4½, 5¼) in / 8.5 (10, 11.5, 13.5) cm long on each side, leaving 10½ (11, 11½, 11¾) in / 27 (28, 29, 30) cm for the neck.
Seam the sides with an invisible seam from the bottom edge up to the markers or scrap yarn; remove the markers/scrap yarn.
Pin lower edge band to lower edge of the sweater, RS to RS. Begin and end at the front, about 3½ in / 9 cm from where the seam will be (= marked with X on the diagram). You'll need to stretch the band a little to compensate for the difference between its 32¼ (35½, 38½, 42½) in / 82 (90, 98, 108) cm and the 34¾ (37¾, 41, 44¾) in / 88 (96, 104, 114) cm of lower edge of sweater.
With wrong sides facing, seam band (see "Tips," page 87), but do not sew the ends of the band together; leave this "dart" open.
Using the tapestry needle, weave in the yarn tail of the lower edge

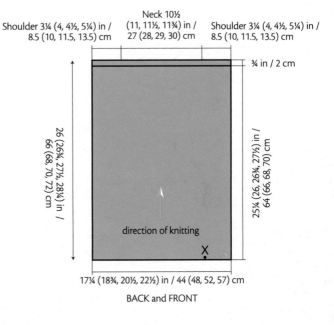

Shoulder 3¼ (4, 4½, 5¼) in / 8.5 (10, 11.5, 13.5) cm

Neck 10½ (11, 11½, 11¾) in / 27 (28, 29, 30) cm

Shoulder 3¼ (4, 4½, 5¼) in / 8.5 (10, 11.5, 13.5) cm

¾ in / 2 cm

26 (26¾, 27¼, 28¼) in / 66 (68, 70, 72) cm

direction of knitting

25¼ (26, 26¾, 27½) in / 64 (66, 68, 70) cm

X

17¼ (18¾, 20½, 22½) in / 44 (48, 52, 57) cm

BACK and FRONT

band along the lower edge and then trim excess yarn.

Bow: CO 25 sts. Work in garter stitch for 2¼ in/6 cm / 11 rows.
BO all sts and cut yarn, leaving a tail approx. 6 in / 15 cm long. This tail can be used in sewing during bow construction.
Fold piece in half; sew the ends together with an invisible seam (see "Tips," page 87) to create a loop. Lay the loop flat with the seam centered at back; wrap the yarn tail several times around the loop and pull tight to create a bow shape. Sew the bow a little above the "dart" in the lower edge band (= marked with X on the diagram). Secure the bow to the sweater by sewing it down in a few additional places.

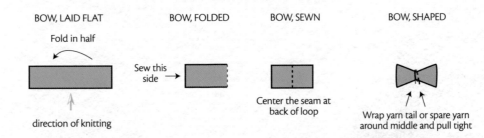

BOW, LAID FLAT
Fold in half
direction of knitting

BOW, FOLDED
Sew this side →

BOW, SEWN
Center the seam at back of loop

BOW, SHAPED
Wrap yarn tail or spare yarn around middle and pull tight

4
Vest

Worked in garter stitch, using Galaxie.

4. Vest

SIZES	S	M	L	XL	XXL
Number of skeins					
GALAXIE Orbite	7	8	9	10	10
from BERGÈRE de France; CYCA #6 (super bulky/roving; 2% polyester, 18% wool, 80% acrylic; 77 yd/70 m / 100 g)					
Needles: U.S.size 11 / 8 mm Notions: 1 clasp, silver (or other suitable metal)					

Stitch used

GARTER STITCH: Knit all rows.

Gauge

It's very important to knit a gauge swatch (see "The Indispensable Gauge," page 86).
10 sts and 20 rows of garter stitch = 4 x 4 in / 10 x 10 cm.
Adjust needle size to obtain correct gauge if necessary.

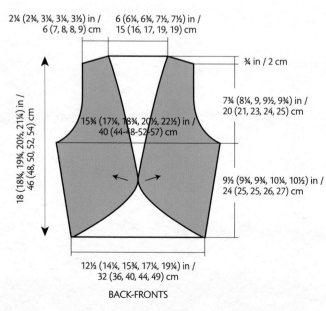

2¼ (2¾, 3¼, 3¼, 3½) in / 6 (7, 8, 8, 9) cm

6 (6¼, 6¾, 7½, 7½) in / 15 (16, 17, 19, 19) cm

¾ in / 2 cm

7¾ (8¼, 9, 9½, 9¾) in / 20 (21, 23, 24, 25) cm

18 (18¾, 19¾, 20½, 21¼) in / 46 (48, 50, 52, 54) cm

15¾ (17¼, 18¾, 20½, 22½) in / 40 (44-48-52-57) cm

9½ (9¾, 9¾, 10¼, 10½) in / 24 (25, 25, 26, 27) cm

12½ (14¼, 15¾, 17¼, 19¼) in / 32 (36, 40, 44, 49) cm

BACK-FRONTS

Instructions

BACK

CO 34 (38, 42, 46, 51) sts. Work in garter stitch, increasing 1 st on each side every 10 rows 4 times = 42 (46, 50, 54, 59) sts.
Continue in garter stitch without further shaping until piece measures 9½ (9¾, 9¾, 10¼, 10½) in/24 (25, 25, 26, 27) cm / 48 (50, 50, 52, 54) rows total.
Armhole shaping: BO 2 sts on each side; then dec 1 st at edge* on every other row:
S and M: 5 times.
L: 6 times.
XL: 7 times.
XXL: 8 times.
*To dec 1 st at edge: K1, k2tog; knit until 3 sts rem; sl 1, k1, psso; k1. After armhole shaping is complete, 28 (32, 34, 36, 39) sts rem. Continue in garter st until armhole depth is approx. 7¾ (8¼, 9, 9½, 9¾) in/20 (21, 23, 24, 25) cm from beg of armhole / after 88 (92, 96, 100, 104) rows total.
Shoulders: At each side on every other row:
S: BO 2 sts twice and then 3 sts once.
M: BO 2 sts once and then 3 sts twice.
L and XL: BO 3 sts 3 times.
XXL: BO 3 sts twice and then 4 sts once.
BO rem 14 (16, 16, 18, 19) sts for the neck.

LEFT FRONT

The arrows on the diagram indicate the direction of knitting.
Loosely CO 52 (56, 60, 64, 68) sts. Work in garter stitch.
After ¾ in/2 cm / 4 rows, k1, k2tog, k20 (22, 24, 26, 28), k2tog, k27 (29, 31, 33, 35) = 50 (54, 58, 62, 66) sts rem.
Knit 3 rows.
On next row, k1, k2tog, k18 (20, 22, 24, 26), k2tog, k27 (29, 31, 33, 35) = 48 (52, 56, 60, 64) sts rem.
Knit 3 rows.
On next row, k1, k2tog, k16 (18, 20, 22, 24), k2tog, k27 (29, 31, 33, 35).

Repeat this dec on every 4th row another:

S: 8 times = 32 sts rem.
M: 9 times = 34 sts rem.
L: 10 times = 36 sts rem.
XL: 11 times = 38 sts rem.
XXL: 12 times 40 sts rem.

Armhole shaping: *At the same time* as working left front decreases, after 2¼ (2¾, 3¼, 3¼, 3½) in/6 (7, 8, 8, 9) cm / 10 (14, 16, 16, 18) rows total, begin short-row shaping. On every other row, knit until N sts (see numbers for each size below) rem and end row (after turning work, yo, slip 1 purlwise, and end row), where N is:

S: 3 sts once, 2 sts 9 times, 1 st 7 times, and 2 rem sts.
M: 4 sts twice, 3 sts once, 2 sts 5 times, 1 st 9 times, and 2 rem sts.
L: 4 sts twice, 3 sts once, 2 sts 6 times, 1 st 9 times, and 2 rem sts.
XL: 4 sts twice, 3 sts once, 2 sts 6 times, 1 st 11 times, and 2 rem sts.
XXL: 4 sts twice, 3 sts once, 2 sts 7 times, 1 st 11 times, and 2 rem sts.

RIGHT FRONT
Work as for left front, reversing shaping.

Finishing

Edge of left armhole: With RS facing, resume working the remaining sts of left front = 30 (34, 38, 42, 46) sts, knitting each yo tog with the st following yo. After these sts have been worked, work across edge of back left armhole, knitting 2 tog across to join 1 side st and 1 bound-off st.
On next row, BO all sts by working k2tog across the front sts until 2 sts rem once, and then work k2tog across the front sts until 4 sts rem twice.

Edge of right armhole: Work as for left side, reversing shaping.
Seam sides of vest.
Sew one half of clasp to each side of vest at the corner created by the decreases (see photo).

5
Short sweater

Worked in pattern stitch,
using Magic +.

5. Short sweater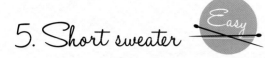

SIZES	S	M	L	XL
	Number of skeins			
MAGIC + Renard	10	11	12	13
from BERGÈRE de France; CYCA #4 (worsted/afghan/aran; 50% wool, 50% acrylic; 87 yd/80 m / 50g)				
Needles: U.S. size 9 / 5.5 mm; 1 tapestry needle (for seaming and weaving in ends)				

Stitches used

PATTERN STITCH A:
Row 1 (RS): Knit.
Row 2: K2, p2 across.
Repeat Rows 1-2 for pattern stitch.

PATTERN STITCH B:
Row 1 (RS): P2, k2 across.
Row 2: Knit.
Repeat Rows 1-2 for pattern stitch.

Gauge

It's very important to knit a gauge swatch (see "The Indispensable Gauge," page 86).
16 sts and 23 rows in Pattern Stitch A or Pattern Stitch B = 4 x 4 in / 10 x 10 cm.
Adjust needle size to obtain correct gauge if necessary.

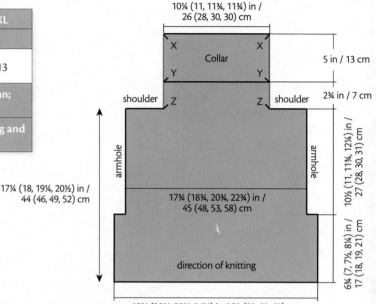

10¼ (11, 11¾, 11¾) in / 26 (28, 30, 30) cm

Collar

5 in / 13 cm

2¾ in / 7 cm

shoulder   shoulder

armhole   armhole

17¼ (18, 19¼, 20½) in / 44 (46, 49, 52) cm

10½ (11, 11¾, 12¼) in / 27 (28, 30, 31) cm

17¾ (18¾, 20¾, 22¾) in / 45 (48, 53, 58) cm

direction of knitting

6¾ (7, 7½, 8¼) in / 17 (18, 19, 21) cm

19¾ (20¾, 22¾, 24¾) in / 50 (53, 58, 63) cm

BACK, FRONT, and COLLAR

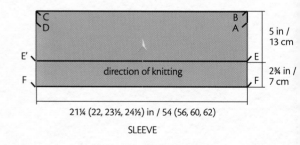

C B
D A

5 in / 13 cm

E'   E

direction of knitting

2¾ in / 7 cm

F   F

21¼ (22, 23½, 24½) in / 54 (56, 60, 62)

SLEEVE

Instructions

BACK

CO 82 (86, 94, 102) sts. Work in Pattern Stitch A for 6¾ (7, 7½, 8¼) in/17 (18, 19, 21) cm / 40 (42, 44, 48) rows.

Armhole shaping: On next row, BO 4 sts (see page 27) and work the rest of the row in Pattern Stitch A = 78 (82, 90, 98) sts rem.

On next row, BO 4 sts and work the rest of the row in Pattern Stitch A = 74 (78, 86, 94) sts rem.

Continue in Pattern Stitch A.

Shoulders: When piece measures 17¼ (18, 19¼, 20½) in/44 (46, 49, 52) cm / 102 (106, 114, 120) rows total, BO 16 (16, 18, 22) sts and then work the rest of the row in Pattern Stitch A = 58 (62, 68, 72) sts rem.

On next row, BO 16 (16, 18, 22) sts and work in pattern to end of row = 42 (46, 50, 50) sts rem.

Collar: Work in Pattern Stitch A for next 13 rows.

On next row (WS), knit across.

Then continue in Pattern Stitch B for 5 in/13 cm / 30 rows, working RS rows:

S and M: as described at beg of pattern.

L and XL: as (k2, p2) across.

On next row, BO all sts (see page 27) and cut yarn, leaving a tail 11¾ in / 30 cm long. The tail can be used in seaming if desired.

FRONT

Work as for back.

SLEEVES

CO 86 (90, 98, 102) sts. Work in Pattern Stitch B for 2¾ in/7 cm / 15 rows.

On next row (WS), (p2, k2) across.

Now continue in Pattern Stitch A for 5 in/13 cm / 30 rows.

BO all sts and cut yarn, leaving a tail 4 in / 10 cm long.

Knit a second sleeve the same way.

Finishing

Join shoulders with an invisible seam (see "Tips," page 87).

Seam sides of the collar with running stitch (see "Tips," page 87) on right side of work from X to Y for the back of collar, and on wrong side of work from Y to Z (see diagram on page 24).

Seam the sleeves to the armholes with an invisible seam, bringing together A and A', B and B', C and C', and D and D' (see diagram below).

Seam the underarm, using running stitch, on wrong side of work from D to E, and then on right side of work from E to F for the back of sleeve (see assembly diagram).

Seam the sides of the sweater with an invisible seam.

Using tapestry needle, weave in the yarn tail along the lower edge and then trim excess yarn.

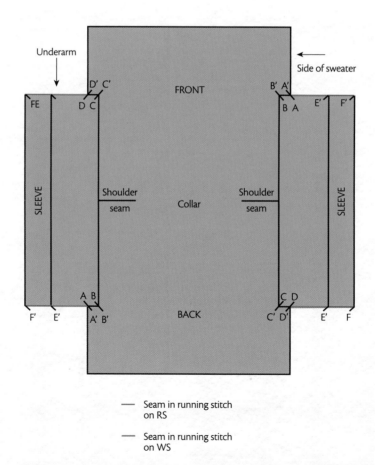

Underarm

Side of sweater

FRONT

D' C'

B' A'

FE

D C

B A

E' F'

SLEEVE

Shoulder

seam

Collar

Shoulder

seam

SLEEVE

F' E'

A B

A' B'

C D

C' D'

E' F

BACK

—— Seam in running stitch on RS

—— Seam in running stitch on WS

Tip

To bind off stitches for armholes:

1. On RS rows: slip 1 stitch purlwise, k1.
With the left needle, pass the slipped stitch over the knit stitch
= 1 stitch has been bound off.
*K1 and pass the stitch on the right needle over this stitch; a
second stitch has been bound off. Repeat from * to BO the
number of stitches indicated.

2. On WS rows, BO the stitches in the same way, but purl
instead of knitting.

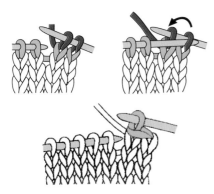

6
Vest with draping collar

Worked in moss stitch, using Cocoon.

6. Vest with draping collar

SIZES	S	M	L	XL	XXL
	Number of skeins				
COCOON Camel	8	9	10	11	12
from BERGÈRE de France; CYCA #5 (chunky/craft/rug; 5% alpaca, 25% mohair, 70% acrylic; 77 yd/70 m / 50 g)					
Needles: U.S. size 10½ / 6.5 mm Notions: 1 brown leather clasp and 2 old gold or brass buttons, one large (25 mm diameter) and one small (14 mm diameter)					

Stitch used

MOSS STITCH:
See page 87.

Gauge

It's very important to knit a gauge swatch (see "The Indispensable Gauge," page 86).
13 sts and 18 rows in moss stitch = 4 x 4 in / 10 x 10 cm.
Adjust needle size to obtain correct gauge if necessary.

Instructions

The vest is made in a single piece, starting with the left front. The arrow on the diagram indicates the direction of knitting.
CO 77 (81, 83, 87, 89) sts. Work in moss stitch.
On Row 3, make a buttonhole: Work the first 62 (65, 67, 70, 72) sts, BO 1 st, and work to end of row.
On next row, CO 1 new st over the bound-off stitch.
Armhole shaping: After 14¼ (15, 15¾, 16¾, 17¾) in/36 (38, 40, 42.5, 45) cm / 64 (68, 72, 76, 82) rows total, the left front is complete.
Back: Work the first 26 (27, 27, 28, 28) sts, BO the next 25 (27, 29, 31, 33) sts, and work to end of row.

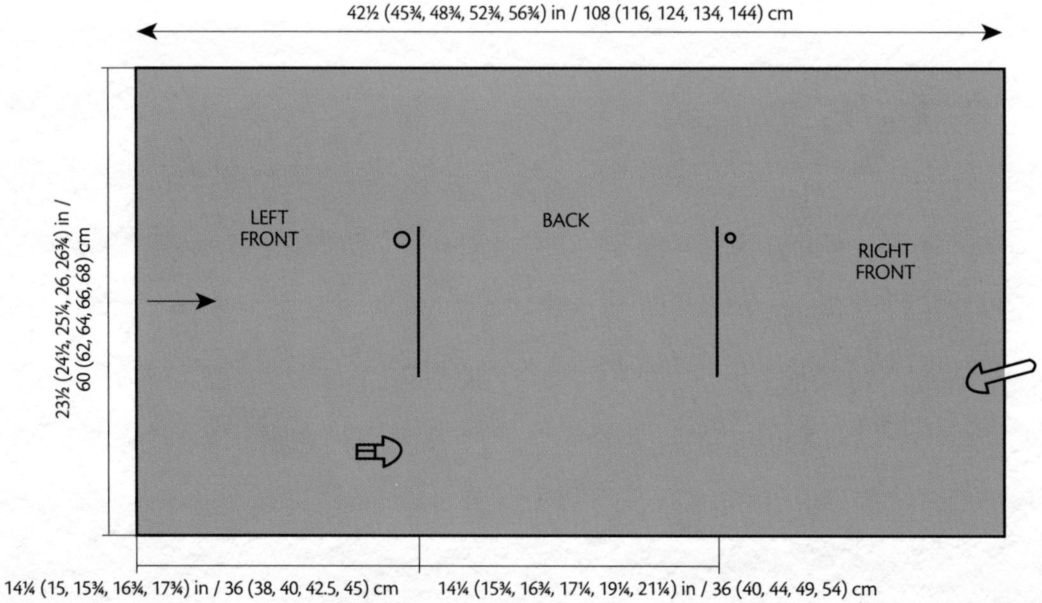
42½ (45¾, 48¾, 52¾, 56¾) in / 108 (116, 124, 134, 144) cm
23½ (24½, 25¼, 26, 26¾) in / 60 (62, 64, 66, 68) cm
LEFT FRONT
BACK
RIGHT FRONT
14¼ (15, 15¾, 16¾, 17¾) in / 36 (38, 40, 42.5, 45) cm
14¼ (15¾, 16¾, 17¼, 19¼, 21¼) in / 36 (40, 44, 49, 54) cm

On next row, CO 25 (27, 29, 31, 33) new sts over the bound-off stitches.

Continue, working across all sts.

Armhole shaping: Approx. 14¼ (15¾, 16¾, 17¼, 19¼, 21¼) in / 36 (40, 44, 49, 54) cm from beg of back / after 130 (140, 152, 166, 178) rows total, work the first 26 (27, 27, 28, 28) sts, BO the next 25 (27, 29, 31, 33) sts, and work to end of row. The back is now complete.

Right front: On next row, CO 25 (27, 29, 31, 33) new sts over the bound-off stitches.

Continue, working across all sts.

Approx. 13¾ (14½, 15¼, 16¼, 17¼) in/35 (37, 39, 41.5, 44) cm from beg of right front / after 192 (206, 222, 240, 258) rows total, make a buttonhole: Work the first 57 (60, 62, 65, 67) sts, BO the next 2 sts, and work to end of row.

On next row, CO 2 new sts over the bound-off stitches.

On next row, the right side is complete; BO all sts.

Finishing

Sew the smaller button to the WS of right front, to the right, about 1½ in / 4 cm down from the top of the armhole and ⅜ in / 1 cm from the edge of the armhole.

Sew the larger button to the RS of left front, about 2¾ in / 7 cm down from the top of the armhole and 2¼ in / 6 cm from the edge of the armhole (see diagram for guidance).

Lay the vest flat, and fold so that the right front lies over the left front; fasten buttons through buttonholes, and then sew on the clasp: Sew the side with the buckle about 4 (4, 4¼, 4¼, 4¾) in / 10 (10, 11, 11, 12) cm from lower edge and about 10½ (11, 11½, 11¾, 12¼) in / 27 (28, 29, 30, 31) cm from side edge of left front. Sew the other half of the clasp at a slight angle, about 7½ (7½, 7¾, 7¾, 8¼) in / 19 (19, 20, 20, 21) cm from lower edge and about 1½ in / 4 cm from side edge of right front.

7
Long cardigan

Worked in pattern stitch and k2, p2
ribbing, using Coton Nature.

7. Long cardigan

SIZES	S	M	L	XL	XXL
	Number of skeins				
COTON NATURE Roc	7	8	9	9	10
COTON NATURE Plâtre	2	2	2	2	3
from BERGÈRE de France; Roc, CYCA #3 (DK/light worsted; 100% cotton; 98 yd/90 m / 50 g), Plâtre, CYCA #1 (sock/fingering/baby; 100% cotton; 207 yd/189 m / 50 g)					
Needles: U.S. size 2.5 / 3 mm					

Stitches used

K2, P2 RIBBING, using Plâtre.

PATTERN STITCH:
Row 1 (RS), Plâtre: Purl.
Row 2, Plâtre: Knit.
Row 3, Roc: * P1, yo *, rep from * to *; end with p1.
Row 4, Roc: * K1, yo, and drop the yo from prev row *, rep from * to *; end with k1.
Row 5, Plâtre: Knit across, dropping the yo from prev row.
Row 6, Plâtre: Knit.
Row 7: Work as for Row 3.

Gauge

It's very important to knit a gauge swatch (see "The Indispensable Gauge," page 86).
16 sts and 16 rows in pattern stitch = 4 x 4 in / 10 x 10 cm.
Adjust needle size to obtain correct gauge if necessary.

Instructions

BACK
CO 76 (82, 90, 96, 104) sts with Roc. Work 1½ in / 4 cm / 12 rows in k2, p2 ribbing.
Continue in pattern stitch until piece measures 18½ (18¾, 18¾, 19¼, 19¾) in/47 (48, 48, 49, 50) cm / 80 (82, 82, 84, 86) rows total.
Armhole shaping: BO 3 sts on each side.
Continue working the rem 70 (76, 84, 90, 98) sts in pattern.
Shoulders and neck: Approx. 7 (7½, 8¼, 8¾, 9) in/18 (19, 21, 22, 23) cm from beg of armhole / after 108 (112, 116, 118, 122) rows total, shape shoulders and neck (see details for beginning neck shaping below): At shoulders, on each side, on every other row:
S: BO 5 sts once, 6 sts 3 times.
M: BO 6 sts 3 times, 7 sts once.
L: BO 7 sts 4 times.
XL: BO 7 sts twice, 8 sts twice.
XXL: BO 8 sts 3 times, 9 sts once.
At the same time as the second decrease for the right shoulder, for the neck, BO the 20 (22, 24, 26, 28) center sts, and work each side separately, binding off 2 sts at neck edge once.

LEFT FRONT
CO 38 (40, 44, 48, 52) sts with Roc. Work 1½ in/4 cm / 12 rows in k2, p2 ribbing, increasing 1 st in Row 12 for sizes M and L = 38 (41, 45, 48, 52) sts.
Continue in pattern stitch until piece measures 40 (41, 41, 42, 43) cm / 68 (70, 70, 72, 74) rows total.
V-neck shaping: Work decreases 2 sts in from left edge. (Work across until 4 sts rem; p2tog, work 2 sts in pattern stitch.)
NOTE: *At the same time* as working neck shaping, when at same length, shape armhole and shoulder as for back.
S: Dec 1 st every 4 rows twice, * 1 st every other row once, 1 st every 4 rows once *, repeat * to * 5 times.
M: Dec 1 st every 4 rows twice, * 1 st every other row once, 1 st every 4 rows once *, repeat * to * 5 times, work one row without decreasing, and then dec 1 st once more.
L: Dec 1 st every 4 rows twice, * 1 st every other row once, 1 st every 4 rows once *, repeat * to * 6 times.

XL: Dec 1 st every 4 rows twice, * 1 st every other row once, 1 st every 4 rows once *, repeat * to * 6 times, work one row without decreasing,
and then dec 1 st once more.

XXL: Dec 1 st every 4 rows twice, * 1 st every other row once, 1 st every 4 rows once *, repeat * to * 7 times.

RIGHT FRONT

Work as for left front, reversing shaping.

Neck decreases:

To dec 1 st 2 sts in from right edge: Work 2 sts in pattern stitch, p2tog, and then complete row.

SLEEVES

CO 42 (44, 46, 46, 48) sts with Roc. Work 3½ in/9 cm / 26 rows in k2, p2 ribbing.

Continue in pattern stitch, increasing on each side 2 sts in from edge as follows:

S: 1 st every 8 rows 4 times, 1 st every 6 rows 5 times = 60 sts.
M: 1 st every 6 rows 10 times = 64 sts.
L: 1 st every 6 rows 8 times, 1 st every 4 rows 4 times = 70 sts.
XL: 1 st every 6 rows 6 times, 1 st every 4 rows 7 times = 72 sts.
XXL: 1 st every 6 rows 4 times, 1 st every 4 rows 10 times = 76 sts.
Continue working in pattern until sleeve measures 20¾ in/53 cm / 96 rows total; work 1¼ in/3 cm / 6 rows in k2, p2 ribbing and then BO.

BANDS FOR FRONT AND NECK (2)

CO 166 (170, 174, 178, 182) sts with Roc. Work 1½ in/4 cm / 12 rows in k2, p2 ribbing and then BO.

Finishing

Join shoulders.

Pin bands to front edges and around neck. Sew on bands and seam short ends of bands at center back neck.

Attach sleeves to armholes, with center of sleeve top at shoulder seam.

Seam sleeves and sides of cardigan.

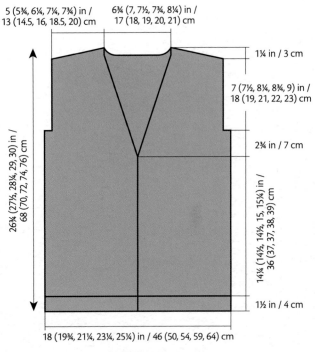

5 (5¾, 6¼, 7¼, 7¾) in / 13 (14.5, 16, 18.5, 20) cm

6¾ (7, 7½, 7¾, 8¼) in / 17 (18, 19, 20, 21) cm

1¼ in / 3 cm

7 (7½, 8¼, 8¾, 9) in / 18 (19, 21, 22, 23) cm

2¾ in / 7 cm

26¾ (27½, 28¼, 29, 30) in / 68 (70, 72, 74, 76) cm

14¼ (14½, 14½, 15, 15¼) in / 36 (37, 37, 38, 39) cm

1½ in / 4 cm

18 (19¾, 21¼, 23¼, 25¼) in / 46 (50, 54, 59, 64) cm

BACK-FRONTS

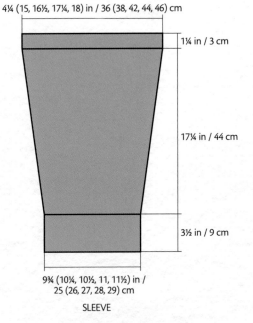

4¼ (15, 16½, 17¼, 18) in / 36 (38, 42, 44, 46) cm

1¼ in / 3 cm

17¼ in / 44 cm

3½ in / 9 cm

9¾ (10¼, 10½, 11, 11½) in / 25 (26, 27, 28, 29) cm

SLEEVE

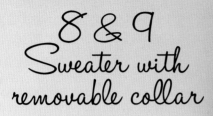

8 & 9
Sweater with removable collar

Worked in garter stitch and St st,
using Plume.

8. Sweater

Easy

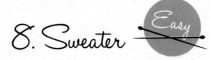

SIZES	S	M	L	XL	XXL
	Number of skeins				
PLUME Néon	12	13	14	16	16
from BERGÈRE de France; CYCA #4 (worsted/afghan/aran; 11% wool, 42% acrylic, 47% polyamide; 87 yd/80 m / 50 g)					
Needles: U.S. sizes 8 and 9 / 5 and 5.5 mm					

Stitches used

GARTER STITCH, using smaller needles: Knit all rows.

STOCKINETTE, using larger needles:
Row 1 (RS): Knit.
Row 2: Purl.
Repeat Rows 1-2.

Gauge

It's very important to knit a gauge swatch (see "The Indispensable Gauge," page 86).
15 sts and 20 rows in St st = 4 x 4 in / 10 x 10 cm.
Adjust needle sizes to obtain correct gauge if necessary.

Instructions

BACK

With smaller needles, CO 83 (89, 95, 103, 110) sts. Work 2 rows in garter stitch.
Change to larger needles and St st, and work 6 more rows.
Row 9: K3, k2tog, k73 (79, 85, 93, 100); sl 1, k1, psso; k3 = 81 (87, 93, 101, 108) sts rem.
Work 9 rows.
On next row, k3, k2tog, k71 (77, 83, 91, 98); sl 1, k1, psso; k3 = 79 (85, 91, 99, 106) sts rem.
Work 9 rows.
Continue, and, on every 10th row, decrease 1 st 3 sts in from edge at each side 7 more times.

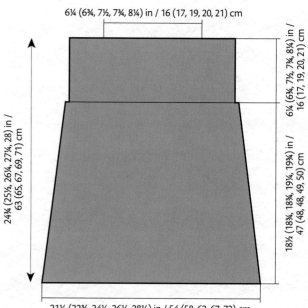

6¼ (6¾, 7½, 7¾, 8¼) in / 16 (17, 19, 20, 21) cm
24¾ (25½, 26¼, 27¼, 28) in / 63 (65, 67, 69, 71) cm
6¼ (6¾, 7½, 7¾, 8¼) in / 16 (17, 19, 20, 21) cm
18½ (18¾, 18¾, 19¼, 19¾) in / 47 (48, 48, 49, 50) cm
21¼ (22¾, 24½, 26¼, 28¼) in / 54 (58, 62, 67, 72) cm
BACK-FRONTS

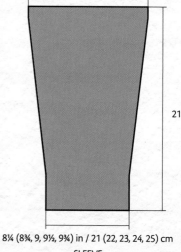

11¾ (12½, 13¾, 14½, 15¼) in / 30 (32, 35, 37, 39) cm
21¼ in / 54 cm
8¼ (8¾, 9, 9½, 9¾) in / 21 (22, 23, 24, 25) cm
SLEEVE

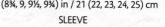

After these decreases are complete, 65 (71, 77, 85, 92) sts rem. Continue in St st until piece measures 18½ (18¾, 18¾, 19¼, 19¾) in/47 (48, 48, 49, 50) cm / 96 (98, 98, 100, 102) rows total.
Armhole shaping: On RS, BO 2 sts and knit to end of row.
On next row, BO 2 sts and purl to end of row = 61 (67, 73, 81, 88) sts rem.
Shoulders and neck: When armhole depth is 6¼ (6¾, 7½, 7¾, 8¼) in/16 (17, 19, 20, 21) cm / after 128 (132, 136, 140, 144) rows total, BO all sts.

FRONT
Work as for back.

SLEEVES
With smaller needles, CO 33 (35, 37, 37, 39) sts. Work 2 rows in garter stitch.
Switch to larger needles and St st; work 20 more rows.
Row 23: K2, inc 1 st, k29 (31, 33, 33, 35), inc 1 st, k2 = 35 (37, 39, 39, 41) sts.
Work 13 (11, 9, 9, 7) rows.
On next row, k2, inc 1 st, k31 (33, 35, 35, 37), inc 1 st, k2 = 37 (39, 41, 41, 43) sts.
Work 13 (11, 9, 9, 7) rows
Repeat the increase row as follows:
S: every 14 rows once, every 12 rows 4 times = 47 sts.
M: every 12 rows twice, every 10 rows 4 times = 51 sts.
L: every 10 rows 7 times = 55 sts.
XL: every 10 rows twice, every 8 rows 6 times = 57 sts.
XXL: every 8 rows 9 times = 61 sts.
When sleeve measures 21¼ in/54 cm / 110 rows total, BO loosely.

Finishing

Join 16 (18, 20, 23, 26) sts from front and from back on each side to form the shoulders.
Sew tops of sleeves to tops of armholes, and then seam sleeves and sides of sweater.
If desired, roll lower edge of sweater and cuffs of sleeves and secure in place with a few small stitches.

9. Removable collar

With larger needles, CO 125 sts. Work 15¾ in/40 cm / 80 rows in St st and then BO.
Sew sides of collar together to create a loop.

10
Shrug

Worked in garter stitch and stockinette,
using Plume.

10. Shrug

SIZES	XS/S 36/40	M 42/48	L/XL 50/54
	Number of skeins		
PLUME Satellite	5	6	7
from BERGÈRE de France; CYCA #4 (worsted/afghan/aran; 11% wool, 42% acrylic, 47% polyamide; 87 yd/80 m / 50 g)			
Needles: U.S. size 9 / 5.5 mm; 1 tapestry needle (for seaming and weaving in ends) and pins for finishing			

Stitches used

GARTER STITCH: Knit all rows.

STOCKINETTE:
Row 1 (RS): Knit.
Row 2: Purl.
Repeat Rows 1-2.

Gauge

It's very important to knit a gauge swatch (see "The Indispensable Gauge," page 86).
15 sts and 20 rows in St st = 4 x 4 in / 10 x 10 cm.
Adjust needle size to obtain correct gauge if necessary.

Instructions

CO 46 (52, 58) sts. Work 3 sts in garter stitch, 40 (46, 52) sts in St st, and 3 sts in garter stitch.
After 15¾ (17¼, 18¾) in/40 (44, 48) cm / 80 (88, 96) rows, place a marker or wind some scrap yarn through the first few stitches (= at B' on the diagram).
Continue, working 3 sts in garter stitch, 40 (46, 52) sts in St st, and 3 sts in garter stitch.
After 27½ (30¾, 33¾) in/70 (78, 86) cm / 140 (156, 172) rows total, place another marker or wind some more scrap yarn through the first few stitches (= at X on the diagram).

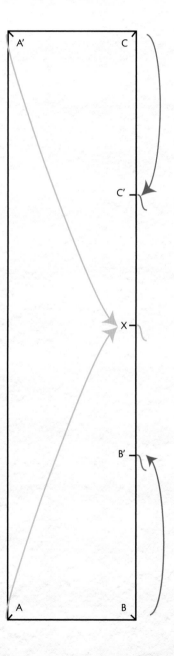

Then continue, still working 3 sts in garter stitch, 40 (46, 52) sts in St st, and 3 sts in garter stitch.

After 39¼ (44, 48¾) in/100 (112, 124) cm / 200 (224, 248) rows total, place another marker or wind some more scrap yarn through the first few stitches (= at C' on the diagram).

Continue, still working 3 sts in garter stitch, 40 (46, 52) sts in St st, and 3 sts in garter stitch.

After 55 (61½, 67¾) in/140 (156, 172) cm / 280 (312, 344) rows total, BO (see page 27) and cut yarn, leaving a tail 4 in / 10 cm long.

Finishing

On WS of work, bring together B and B' (see diagram) and pin in place, making sure the pin secures both layers. Bring together A and X and pin in place the same way.

With the tapestry needle and running stitch, seam the length between the pins (from BB' to AX).

On WS of work, bring together C and C' and pin in place, making sure the pin secures both layers. Bring together A' and X and pin in place the same way.

With the tapestry needle and running stitch, seam the length between the pins (from CC' to A'X).

Remove the markers/lengths of scrap yarn.

Using tapestry needle, weave in the yarn tail along the lower edge and then cut excess yarn.

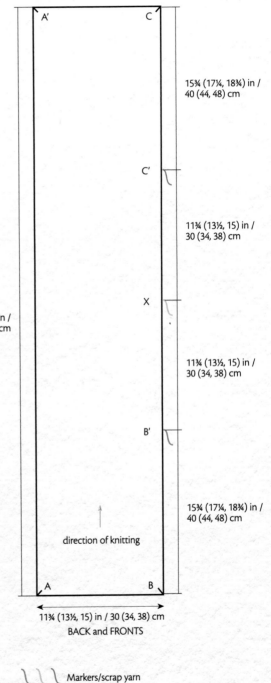

55 (61½, 67¾) in / 140 (156, 172) cm

15¾ (17¼, 18¾) in / 40 (44, 48) cm

11¾ (13½, 15) in / 30 (34, 38) cm

11¾ (13½, 15) in / 30 (34, 38) cm

15¾ (17¼, 18¾) in / 40 (44, 48) cm

direction of knitting

11¾ (13½, 15) in / 30 (34, 38) cm
BACK and FRONTS

ﻮﻮﻮ   Markers/scrap yarn

Raphaëlle

*Color, warmth, gladness …
Using openwork stitches
to play with patterning
and lovely, intricate
details sets these
elegant, feminine
designs apart!*

11
Short cape

Worked in an openwork stitch, with garter
stitch, stockinette, and pattern ribbing,
using Angel.

11. Short cape

SIZES	S/M 38/46	L/XL 48/54
	Number of skeins	
ANGEL Tamaya	3	4
from BERGÈRE de France; CYCA #1 (sock/fingering/baby; 24% mohair, 32% acrylic, 44% polyamide; 601 yd/550 m / 50 g)		
Needles: U.S.sizes 4, 6, and 7 / 3.5, 4, and 4.5 mm		

Stitches used

GARTER STITCH, using U.S. 4 / 3.5 mm needles: Knit all rows.

STOCKINETTE, using U.S. 6 / 4 mm needles:
Row 1 (RS): Knit.
Row 2: Purl.
Repeat Rows 1-2.

OPENWORK STITCH, using U.S. 6 / 4 mm needles. Worked across a multiple of 6 stitches.
Row 1 (RS): K1, * k2tog, 2 yo, sl 1, k1, psso, k2 *; rep from * to * and end with k1 (instead of k2).
Row 2 and all even-numbered rows: Purl across, purling the first of each pair of yarnovers normally and purling the second with a twisted purl (p1-tb1).
Row 3: * K2tog, yo, k2, yo, sl 1, k1, psso *; rep from * to *.
Row 5: K1, * yo, sl 1, k1, psso, k2tog, yo, k2 *; rep from * to * and end with k1 (instead of k2).
Row 7: * Sl 1, k1, psso, k1, 2 yo, k1, k2tog *; rep from * to *.
Row 9: Yo, * sl 1, k1, psso, k2, k2tog, 2 yo *; rep from * to * and end with 1 yo (instead of 2 yo).
Row 11: Work as for Row 5.
Row 13: Work as for Row 3.
Row 15: Yo, k1, k2tog, * sl 1, k1, psso, k1, 2 yo, k1, k2tog *; rep from * to * and end with sl 1, k1, psso, k1, yo.
Row 17: Work as for Row 1.
Repeat Rows 1-18.

PATTERN RIBBING, using U.S. 4 / 3.5 mm needles. Worked across a multiple of 4 + 2 stitches. *To C2 over 2 right:* slip the first 2 sts to the right needle. Drop next 2 sts. Return the 2 slipped sts to the left

OPENWORK STITCH

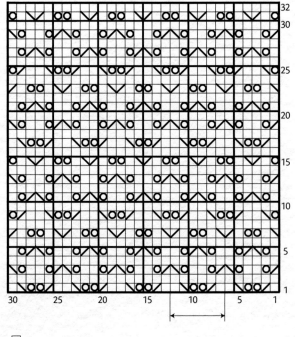

☐ 1 st in stockinette

◢ k2tog

◘ yo

◣ sl 1, k1, psso

needle, and then return the 2 dropped sts to the left needle. K2, p2 over these 4 sts.
Row 1 (RS): * P2, C2 over 2 right *; rep from * to * and end with p2.
Row 2: * K2, p2 *; rep from * to * and end with k2.
Repeat Rows 1-2.

Gauge

It's very important to knit a gauge swatch (see The Indispensable Gauge, page 86).
24 sts and 30 rows in St st on U.S. size 6 / 4 mm needles = 4 x 4 in / 10 x 10 cm.
Adjust needle sizes to obtain correct gauge if necessary.

Instructions

BACK

With U.S. size 7 / 4.5 mm needles, CO 230 (246) sts. Change to U.S. size 4 / 3.5 mm needles and work 2 rows in garter stitch.

Change to U.S. size 6 / 4 mm needles and work 2 rows in St st.

Next row: K1, * work 30 sts in openwork stitch, k27 (31) *; rep from * to * and end with k28 (32) instead of k27 (31).

Work 9 rows the same way, alternating sections of openwork stitch with St st across the row.

Next row: K1, * work 30 sts in openwork stitch, k2, k2tog, k19 (23), k2tog, k2 *; rep from * to * and end with k3 (instead of k2) = 8 decreases.

Work 9 rows without decreasing, alternating sections of openwork stitch with St st across the 222 (238) sts rem.

Next row: K1, * work 30 sts in openwork stitch, k2, k2tog, k17 (21), k2tog, k2 *; rep from * to * and end with k3 (instead of k2) = 8 decreases.

Work 9 rows without decreasing, alternating sections of openwork stitch with St st across the 214 (230) sts rem.

Decrease the same way again:

S/M: every 8th row 8 times.

L/XL: every 10th row once, and then every 8th row 8 times.

After all decrease rows have been worked, continue, alternating sections of openwork stitch with St st across the 150 (158) sts rem.

After 12½ (13¾) in/32 (35) cm / 96 (106) rows total, change to U.S. size 4 / 3.5 mm needles and pattern ribbing.

After 13½ (14½) in/34 (37) cm / 104 (114) rows total, BO 1 st at each side on every 4th row 5 times = 140 (148) sts rem.

Next row: Knit the knits and p2tog with each pair of purls.

Next row: BO the rem 106 (112) sts knitwise.

FRONT

Work as for back.

Finishing

Seam sides of cape.

12 & 13
Short poncho and matching cowl

Worked in garter stitch and pattern ribbing, using Duvetine.

12. Short poncho

SIZES	XS/M	L/XXL
	Number of skeins	
Poncho DUVETINE Lagon	10	12
Snood DUVETINE Lagon	4	4
from BERGÈRE de France; CYCA #5 (chunky/craft/rug; 8% polyester, 19% polyamide, 73% acrylic; 77 yd/70 m / 50 g)		
Needles: U.S. size 10½ / 6.5 mm		

Stitches used

GARTER STITCH: Knit all rows.

PATTERN RIBBING. Worked across an odd number of stitches.
Row 1 (RS): * P1, k1 *, rep from * to * and end with p1.
Row 2: Knit across.
Repeat Rows 1-2.

Gauge

It's very important to knit a gauge swatch (see "The Indispensable Gauge," page 86).
13 sts and 16 rows in pattern ribbing = 4 x 4 in / 10 x 10 cm.
Adjust needle size to obtain correct gauge if necessary.

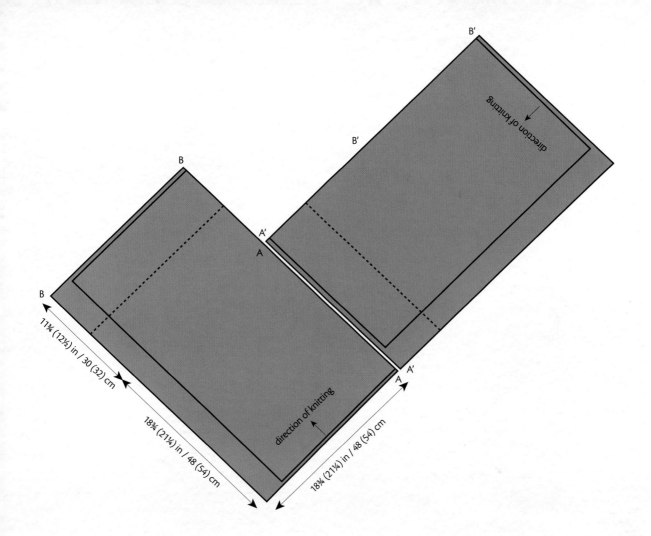

Diagram labels:

B'

direction of knitting

B'

A'

A

B

11¾ (12½) in / 30 (32) cm

18¾ (21¼) in / 48 (54) cm

direction of knitting

B

A' A

18¾ (21¼) in / 48 (54) cm

Instructions

PONCHO

CO 63 (71) sts. Work 2 rows in garter stitch.

Next row: Work 55 (63) sts in pattern ribbing, 8 sts in garter stitch. Continue, working pattern ribbing over pattern ribbing and garter stitch over garter stitch.

After 30¼ (33½) in/77 (85) cm / 124 (138) rows total, work 3 rows in garter stitch across and then BO all sts knitwise.

Work a second piece the same way.

Join the rectangles, bringing together A and A', B and B' (see diagram), and seam.

13. Cowl

CO 46 sts. Work in garter stitch until work measures 33 in / 84 cm total and then BO.

Fold in half so short sides meet, and sew short edges together to form a loop.

14
Open-front collared jacket

Worked in garter stitch, using Teddy.

14. Open-front collared jacket

SIZES	XS	S	M	L	XL	XXL
	Number of skeins					
TEDDY Dumbo	11	12	13	14	16	17
from BERGÈRE de France; CYCA #5 (chunky/craft/rug; 100% polyamide; 88 yd/80 m / 50 g)						
Needles: U.S. size 6 / 4 mm Notions: 1 button						

Stitch used

GARTER STITCH: Knit all rows.

Gauge

It's very important to knit a gauge swatch (see "The Indispensable Gauge," page 86).
16 sts and 32 rows in garter stitch = 4 x 4 in / 10 x 10 cm.
Adjust needle size to obtain correct gauge if necessary.

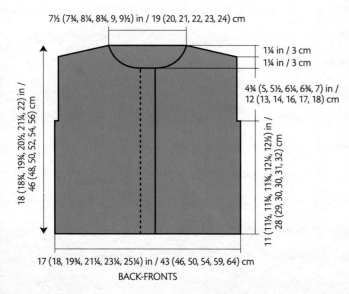

7½ (7¾, 8¼, 8¾, 9, 9½) in / 19 (20, 21, 22, 23, 24) cm

1¼ in / 3 cm
1¼ in / 3 cm

4¾ (5, 5½, 6¼, 6¾, 7) in / 12 (13, 14, 16, 17, 18) cm

18 (18¾, 19¾, 20½, 21¼, 22) in / 46 (48, 50, 52, 54, 56) cm

11 (11½, 11¾, 11¾, 12¼, 12½) in / 28 (29, 30, 30, 31, 32) cm

17 (18, 19¾, 21¼, 23¼, 25¼) in / 43 (46, 50, 54, 59, 64) cm
BACK-FRONTS

Instructions

The wrong and right sides of a piece done in garter stitch are identical; use any sort of marker you like to identify the right side of work for yourself.

BACK
CO 70 (74, 82, 88, 96, 104) sts.
Work in garter stitch until piece measures 11 (11½, 11¾, 11¾, 12¼, 12½) in/28 (29, 30, 30, 31, 32) cm / 90 (92, 96, 96, 100, 102) rows total.
Armhole shaping: BO 2 sts and knit to end of row.
On next row, BO 2 sts and knit to end of row.
Continue in garter st over the rem 66 (70, 78, 84, 92, 100) sts.
Shoulders: After a total of 17 (17¾, 18½, 19¼, 20, 20¾) in/43 (45, 47, 49, 51, 53) cm / 138 (144, 150, 158, 164, 170) rows, shape shoulders:
XS: BO 3 sts each at beg of next 12 rows.
S: BO 3 sts each at beg of next 10 rows and then 4 sts each at beg of next 2 rows.
M: BO 3 sts each at beg of next 2 rows and then 4 sts each at beg of next 10 rows.
L: BO 4 sts each at beg of next 10 rows and then 5 sts each at beg of next 2 rows.
XL: BO 4 sts each at beg of next 4 rows and then 5 sts each at beg of next 8 rows.
XXL: BO 5 sts each at beg of next 10 rows and then 6 sts each at beg of next 2 rows.
On next row, BO the rem 30 (32, 32, 34, 36, 38) sts for the neck.

LEFT FRONT
CO 39 (41, 45, 48, 52, 56) sts.
Work in garter stitch until piece measures 11 (11½, 11¾, 11¾, 12¼, 12½) in/28 (29, 30, 30, 31, 32) cm / 90 (92, 96, 96, 100, 102) rows total.
Armhole shaping: With RS facing, BO 2 sts and knit to end of row.
Continue in garter st over the rem 37 (39, 43, 46, 50, 54) sts.
Neck shaping: After 15¾ (16½, 17¼, 18, 18¾, 19¾) in/40 (42, 44, 46, 48, 50) cm / 128 (134, 140, 148, 154, 160) rows total, with WS facing, BO 9 (10, 10, 11, 12, 13) sts at beg of row, 4 sts at beg of next WS row, 3 sts at beg of next WS row, 2 sts at beg of next WS row, and then 1 st at beg of next WS row.

Continue, working the rem 18 (19, 23, 25, 28, 31) sts in garter st.
Shoulder: After 17 (17¾, 18½, 19¼, 20, 20¾) in/43 (45, 47, 49, 51, 53) cm / 138 (144, 150, 158, 164, 170) rows total, shape shoulder:
XS: BO 3 sts each at beg of next 6 RS rows.
S: BO 3 sts each at beg of next 5 RS rows, and then 4 sts at beg of next RS row.
M: BO 3 sts at beg of next RS row, and then 4 sts each at beg of next 5 RS rows.
L: BO 4 sts each at beg of each of next 5 RS rows, and then 5 sts at beg of next RS row.
XL: BO 4 sts each at beg of next 2 RS rows, and then 5 sts each at beg of next 4 RS rows.
XXL: BO 5 sts each at beg of next 5 RS rows, and then 6 sts at beg of next RS row.

RIGHT FRONT

Begin as for left front.
Armhole shaping: When at same length, shape armhole as for left front, but on WS of work rather than RS.
Continue in garter st over the rem 37 (39, 43, 46, 50, 54) sts.
Neck shaping: When at same length, shape neck as for left front, but on RS of work rather than WS.
Continue, working the rem 18 (19, 23, 25, 28, 31) sts.
Shoulder: When at same length, shape shoulder as for left front, but on WS of work rather than RS.

SLEEVES

CO 50 (54, 56, 64, 66, 70) sts.
Work in garter stitch until sleeve measures 19¼ (19¼, 19¾, 19¾, 19¾, 19¾) in/49 (49, 50, 50, 50, 50) cm / 156 (156, 160, 160, 160, 160) rows total. BO loosely.

COLLAR

CO 104 (107, 110, 113, 116, 119) sts.
Work in garter stitch.
After 1¼ in/3 cm / 10 rows total, make a buttonhole = k4, BO next 3 sts, and knit to end of row.
On next row, work to bound-off sts, CO 3 new sts, and knit to end of row.
After 3½ in/9 cm / 28 rows total, make another buttonhole.
After 4¾ in/12 cm / 38 rows total, BO loosely.

Finishing

Join shoulders.
Pin collar along the length of stitches for neck (the side with buttonholes should be over the right front) and join; fold in half, and secure fold with a few stitches tacking edges of collar to left and right front.
Pin sleeves along the length of the top side of armhole and join.
Seam sleeves and sides of jacket.
Sew on the button.

19¼ (19¼, 19¾, 19¾, 19¾, 19¾) in /
49 (49, 50, 50, 50, 50) cm

11¾ (12½, 13¼, 15, 15¾, 16½) in /
30 (32, 34, 38, 40, 42) cm
SLEEVE

15
Convertible jacket

Worked in stockinette, using Cocoon.

As a vest

As a scarf

As a shrug

57

15. Convertible jacket

SIZES	S to L, 36 to 46	XL/XXL, 48 to 54
	Number of skeins	
COCOON Abîme	11	13
from BERGÈRE de France; CYCA #5 (chunky/craft/rug; 5% alpaca, 25% mohair, 70% acrylic; 77 yd/70 m / 50 g)		
Needles: U.S. size 11 / 8 mm Notions: 1 tapestry needle (for weaving in ends); 18 buttons in a matching color, 1 in / 25 mm in diameter		

Stitch used

STOCKINETTE.
Row 1 (RS): Knit.
Row 2: Purl.
Repeat Rows 1-2.

Gauge

It's very important to knit a gauge swatch (see "The Indispensable Gauge," page 86).
12 sts and 15 rows in St st = 4 x 4 in / 10 x 10 cm.
Adjust needle size to obtain correct gauge if necessary.

Instructions

The finished piece will be about 16½ (18½) in / 42 (47) cm wide and 82¾ (86½) in / 210 (220) cm long.
CO 51 (57) sts. Work in St st for 4 rows.
For help with the yarnover and decrease stitches, see page 61.
– **Row 5:** At left, make a buttonhole—work across until 4 sts rem, yo, k2tog, k2.
– Work 17 rows in St st.
– **Next row:** At left, make a buttonhole—work across until 4 sts rem, yo, k2tog, k2.
– Work 17 rows in St st.
– **Next row:** At left, make a buttonhole—work across until 4 sts rem, yo, k2tog, k2.
– Work 17 rows in St st.
– **Next row:** At right, make a buttonhole—beg row with k2, sl 1, k1, psso, yo, and then complete row.
– Work 17 rows in St st.
– **Next row:** At right, make a buttonhole—beg row with k2, sl 1, k1, psso, yo, and then complete row.
– Work 17 rows in St st.
– **Next row:** At right, make a buttonhole—beg row with k2, sl 1, k1, psso, yo, and then complete row.
– Work 17 rows in St st.
– **Next row:** At right, make a buttonhole—beg row with k2, sl 1, k1, psso, yo, and then complete row.
– Work 23½ (27½) in/60 (70) cm / 89 (105) rows in St st.
– **Next row:** At left, make a buttonhole—work across until 4 sts rem, yo, k2tog, k2.
– Work 17 rows in St st.
– **Next row:** At left, make a buttonhole—work across until 4 sts rem, yo, k2tog, k2.
– Work 17 rows in St st.
– **Next row:** At left, make a buttonhole—work across until 4 sts rem, yo, k2tog, k2.
– Work 17 rows in St st.
– **Next row:** At left, make a buttonhole—work across until 4 sts rem, yo, k2tog, k2.
– Work 17 rows in St st.

direction of knitting

● button
○ buttonhole

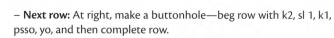

– **Next row:** At right, make a buttonhole—beg row with k2, sl 1, k1, psso, yo, and then complete row.
– Work 17 rows in St st.
– **Next row:** At right, make a buttonhole—beg row with k2, sl 1, k1, psso, yo, and then complete row.
– Work 17 rows in St st.
– **Next row:** At right, make a buttonhole—beg row with k2, sl 1, k1, psso, yo, and then complete row.
– Work 2 rows in St st.
– **Next row (WS):** BO all sts knitwise (see page 27) and cut yarn, leaving a tail 4 in / 10 cm long.
Using the tapestry needle, weave in the yarn tail along the lower edge and then cut excess yarn.
Sew on buttons opposite buttonholes (see diagram, page 59).
When wearing this jacket, you can button it one of several different ways, or leave it unbuttoned (see photos).

YARNOVER

Hold the yarn in front of the work and pass it over the right needle.

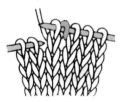

The yarnover forms a stitch on the right needle, with a small opening at the base.

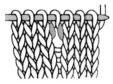

On next row, work the yarnover like any other stitch. It forms an additional stitch—the reverse of a decrease like k2tog or sl 1, k1, psso.

KNIT TWO TOGETHER (k2tog)

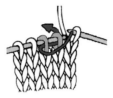

Slide the right needle into the second stitch on the left needle, and then the first.

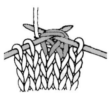

Wrap the yarn around the right needle and bring through both stitches at once.

After a k2tog, the number of stitches has decreased by one.

SLIP 1, KNIT 1, PASS THE SLIPPED STITCH OVER (Sl 1, k1, psso)

Slip a stitch to the right needle, as for a knit stitch. Knit the next stitch.

With the left needle, lift the slipped stitch and pass it over the knitted stitch.

After a sl 1, k1, psso, the number of stitches has decreased by one.

16
Short cardigan

Worked in stockinette and k1, p1 ribbing, using Angel.

16. Short cardigan — *Easy*

SIZES	S	M	L	XL	XXL
	Number of skeins				
ANGEL Violette	3	3	4	4	4
from BERGÈRE de France; CYCA #1 (sock/fingering/baby; 24% mohair, 32% acrylic, 44% polyamide; 601 yd/550 m / 50 g)					
Needles: U.S.sizes 2.5 and 4 / 3 and 3.5 mm Notions: 3 buttons					

Stitches used

K1, P1 RIBBING, using smaller needles:
Row 1 (RS): (K1, p1).
Row 2: Work knit over knit and purl over purl.
Repeat Rows 1-2.

STOCKINETTE, using larger needles:
Row 1 (RS): Knit.
Row 2: Purl.
Repeat Rows 1-2.

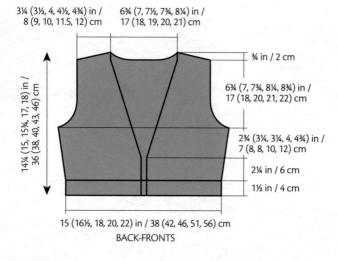

3¼ (3½, 4, 4½, 4¾) in / 8 (9, 10, 11.5, 12) cm

6¾ (7, 7½, 7¾, 8¼) in / 17 (18, 19, 20, 21) cm

¾ in / 2 cm

6¾ (7, 7¾, 8¼, 8¾) in / 17 (18, 20, 21, 22) cm

2¾ (3¼, 3¼, 4, 4¾) in / 7 (8, 8, 10, 12) cm

2¼ in / 6 cm

1½ in / 4 cm

14¼ (15, 15¾, 17, 18) in / 36 (38, 40, 43, 46) cm

15 (16½, 18, 20, 22) in / 38 (42, 46, 51, 56) cm
BACK-FRONTS

Gauge

It's very important to knit a gauge swatch (see "The Indispensable Gauge," page 86).
28 sts and 35 rows in St st (on larger needles) = 4 x 4 in / 10 x 10 cm.
Adjust needle sizes to obtain correct gauge if necessary.

Instructions

BACK

With smaller needles, CO 109 (119, 131, 145, 159) sts. Work 1½ in/4 cm / 18 rows in k1, p1 ribbing. Change to larger needles and St st, *at the same time* increasing on each side:
S, M, and L: 1 st every 8 rows twice, 1 st every 6 rows 4 times.
XL: 1 st every 8 rows 6 times.
XXL: 1 st every 10 rows 3 times, 1 st every 8 rows 3 times.
Continue in St st over 121 (131, 143, 157, 171) sts until piece measures 6¾ (7, 7, 7¾, 8¾) in/17 (18, 18, 20, 22) cm / 64 (68, 68, 74, 82) rows total.
Armhole shaping: At each side, on every other row:
S: BO 3 sts once, 2 sts 3 times, and then 1 st 4 times = 95 sts rem.
M: BO 3 sts once, 2 sts 3 times, and then1 st 5 times = 103 sts rem.
L: BO 3 sts once, 2 sts 4 times, and then 1 st 5 times = 111 sts rem.
XL: BO 3 sts twice, 2 sts 3 times, and then 1 st 5 times = 123 sts rem.
XXL: BO 3 sts twice, 2 sts 5 times, and then 1 st 5 times = 129 sts rem.
Continue in St st until armhole depth is 6¾ (7, 7¾, 8¼, 8¾) in/17 (18, 20, 21, 22) cm / after 124 (132, 138, 148, 160) rows total.
Shoulders and neck: *At the same time* as first shoulder dec, BO the 37 (39, 43, 47, 49) center sts for neck and work each side separately. At shoulder, shape as follows, and, *at the same time*, at neck edge, BO 3 sts and on next alternate row, BO 2 sts.
On every other row at shoulder:
S: BO 6 sts 4 times
M: BO 6 sts once and then 7 sts 3 times.
L: BO 7 sts 3 times and then 8 sts once.
XL: BO 8 sts 3 times and then 9 sts once.
XXL: BO 8 sts once and then 9 sts 3 times.

RIGHT FRONT

With smaller needles, CO 51 (57, 63, 69, 77) sts. Work 1½ in/4 cm / 18 rows in k1, p1 ribbing. Change to larger needles and St st, *at the same time* increasing 1 st on first row of St st for Sizes S and XL (= 52 (57, 63, 70, 77) sts) and increasing on left side only as for back = 58 (63, 69, 76, 83) sts.
Neck shaping: After 4 in/10 cm / 40 rows total, dec 1 st at right side, 2 sts in from edge on every 4th row (= k2, k2tog, and then complete row):
S: 21 times.
M: 22 times.
L: 24 times.

XL: 26 times.

XXL: 27 times.

After armhole and neck shaping, 24 (27, 29, 33, 35) sts rem for shoulder.

Armhole and shoulder: When at same length as for back, shape armhole and shoulder as for back.

LEFT FRONT

Work as for right front, reversing shaping.

Neck decreases: Work across until 4 sts rem; end row with sl 1, k1, psso, k2.

SLEEVES

With smaller needles, CO 75 (81, 89, 97, 105) sts. Work 1½ in/4 cm / 18 rows in k1, p1 ribbing. Change to larger needles and St st, *at the same time* increasing 1 st on *each* side 2 sts in from edge every 8 rows 3 times, and then every 6 rows 3 times = 87 (93, 101, 109, 117) sts.

Continue in St st until work measures 7 in/18 cm / 68 rows total.

Sleeve cap: At each side, on every other row:

S: BO 3 sts once, 2 sts 4 times, 1 st 13 times, 2 sts 4 times, 3 sts once, and then all 17 sts rem.

M: BO 3 sts once, 2 sts 5 times, 1 st 11 times, 2 sts 4 times, 3 sts twice, and then all 17 sts rem.

L: BO 3 sts once, 2 sts 6 times, 1 st 11 times, 2 sts 5 times, 3 sts twice, and then all 17 sts rem.

XL: BO 3 sts twice, 2 sts 5 times, 1 st 12 times, 2 sts 6 times, 3 sts twice, and then all 17 sts rem.

XXL: BO 3 sts twice, 2 sts 6 times, 1 st 9 times, 2 sts 7 times, 3 sts 3 times, and then all 17 sts rem.

BANDS FOR FRONT AND NECK (2)

With smaller needles, CO 159 (169, 179, 191, 205) sts. Work 8 rows in k1, p1 ribbing. For right front band, on Row 4, make 3 buttonholes 1 stitch wide—the first 5 sts in from edge, the second 11 sts in from the first, and the third 11 sts in from the second.

Make left front band the same way, without buttonholes.

Finishing

Join shoulders.

Pin the 2 front bands to front edge, and then sew them so they run up front edges and around to center back neck; seam band ends together at center back neck.

Attach sleeves with center of sleeve cap at shoulder seam. Seam sleeves and sides of cardigan.

Sew on buttons opposite buttonholes.

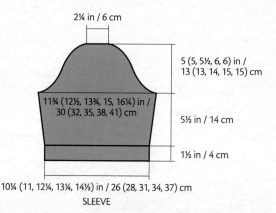

2¼ in / 6 cm

5 (5, 5½, 6, 6) in /
13 (13, 14, 15, 15) cm

11¾ (12½, 13¾, 15, 16¼) in /
30 (32, 35, 38, 41) cm

5½ in / 14 cm

1½ in / 4 cm

10¼ (11, 12¼, 13¼, 14½) in / 26 (28, 31, 34, 37) cm

SLEEVE

17
Short-sleeved cardigan

Worked in stockinette,
k1, p1 ribbing and k2, p2 ribbing,
using Sirène and Angel.

17. Short-sleeved cardigan

SIZES	S	M	L	XL	XXL
	Number of skeins				
SIRÈNE Rocher	5	6	6	7	8
ANGEL Pavé	3	3	4	4	4
from BERGÈRE de France; Sirène, CYCA #1 (sock/fingering/baby; 100% polyamide; 208 yd/190 m / 50 g), Angel, CYCA #1 (sock/fingering/baby; 24% mohair, 32% acrylic, 44% polyamide; 601 yd/550 m / 50 g)					
Needles: U.S. sizes 4 and 7 / 3.5 and 4.5 mm					

Stitches used

Work with 1 strand SIRÈNE and 1 strand ANGEL held together throughout. Make sure each yarn is visible at fairly regular intervals.
K2, P2 RIBBING, using smaller needles.

K1, P1 RIBBING, using smaller needles.

STOCKINETTE, using larger needles:
Row 1 (RS): Knit.
Row 2: Purl.
Repeat Rows 1-2.

Gauge

It's very important to knit a gauge swatch (see "The Indispensable Gauge," page 86).
23 sts and 28 rows in St st = 4 x 4 in / 10 x 10 cm.
Adjust needle sizes to obtain correct gauge if necessary.

Instructions

Please read through all instructions carefully, as shaping at sides varies on each side.
BACK
With smaller needles, CO 92 (100, 108, 118, 128) sts. Work 4¼ in/11 cm / 36 rows in k2, p2 ribbing.
Change to larger needles and St st.

Yoke shaping: After 10¼ (10½, 11, 11, 11½) in/26 (27, 28, 28, 29) cm / 78 (82, 84, 84, 88) rows total, BO 2 (2, 3, 3, 3) sts on each side once and then dec 1 st, 3 sts in from edge on each side (= k3, k2tog, work across until 5 sts rem, sl 1, k1, psso, k3) as follows:
S: 1 st every 4 rows 5 times, 1 st every other row 24 times.
M: 1 st every 4 rows 4 times, 1 st every other row 27 times.
L: 1 st every 4 rows 4 times, 1 st every other row 29 times.
XL: 1 st every 4 rows 3 times, 1 st every other row 34 times.
XXL: 1 st every other row 41 times.
Next row: BO the rem 30 (34, 36, 38, 40) sts.

LEFT FRONT
With smaller needles, CO 34 (38, 42, 48, 52) sts. Work 4¼ in/11 cm / 36 rows in k2, p2 ribbing. Change to larger needles and St st, *at the same time* decreasing 1 st on first row of St st on Size L only = 34 (38, 42, 47, 52) sts.
Yoke and neck: After 10¼ (10½, 11, 11, 11½) in/26 (27, 28, 28, 29) cm / 78 (82, 84, 84, 88) rows total, work shaping on right and left sides as follows:

At right side, BO 2 (2, 2, 3, 3, 3) sts and then dec 1 st at right side, 3 sts in from edge the same way as for back, but with 10 fewer decreases:
S: 1 st every 4 rows 5 times, 1 st every other row 14 times.
M: 1 st every 4 rows 4 times, 1 st every other row 17 times.
L: 1 st every 4 rows 4 times, 1 st every other row 19 times.
XL: 1 st every 4 rows 3 times, 1 st every other row 24 times.
XXL: 1 st every other row 31 times.
At the same time, at left side, dec 1 st 1 st in from edge (= work across until 3 sts rem, sl 1, k1, psso, k1):
S: every 4 rows 6 times, every 6 rows 3 times.
M: every 4 rows 11 times.
L: every 4 rows 12 times.
XL: every 4 rows 13 times.
XXL: every 4 rows 14 times.
After the last decrease, BO rem 4 sts.

RIGHT FRONT
Work as for left front, reversing shaping. For neck decreases: Beg row with k1, k2tog, and then work across.

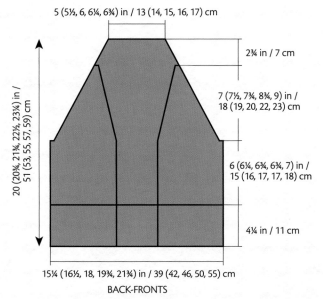

5 (5½, 6, 6¼, 6¾) in / 13 (14, 15, 16, 17) cm

2¾ in / 7 cm

7 (7½, 7¾, 8¾, 9) in / 18 (19, 20, 22, 23) cm

20 (20¾, 21¼, 22½, 23¼) in / 51 (53, 55, 57, 59) cm

6 (6¼, 6¾, 6¾, 7) in / 15 (16, 17, 17, 18) cm

4¼ in / 11 cm

15¼ (16½, 18, 19¾, 21¾) in / 39 (42, 46, 50, 55) cm

BACK-FRONTS

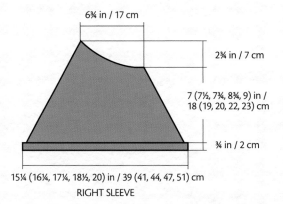

6¾ in / 17 cm

2¾ in / 7 cm

7 (7½, 7¾, 8¾, 9) in / 18 (19, 20, 22, 23) cm

¾ in / 2 cm

15¼ (16¼, 17¼, 18½, 20) in / 39 (41, 44, 47, 51) cm

RIGHT SLEEVE

RIGHT SLEEVE

With smaller needles, CO 92 (96, 102, 110, 118) sts. Work ¾ in/2 cm / 8 rows in k2, p2 ribbing.

Yoke shaping: Change to larger needles and St st, *at the same time* binding off on each side of first row of St st 2 (2, 3, 3, 3) sts.
Continue, decreasing 3 sts in from edge, on *each* side, as for front:
S: 1 st every 4 rows 5 times, 1 st every other row 14 times.
M: 1 st every 4 rows 4 times, 1 st every other row 17 times.
L: 1 st every 4 rows 4 times, 1 st every other row 19 times.
XL: 1 st every 4 rows 3 times, 1 st every other row 24 times.
XXL: 1 st every other row 31 times.

Next, at right side, on every other row: BO 11 sts once, 5 sts once, 3 sts 4 times, 2 sts 4 times, and then all 4 sts rem.
At the same time, at left side, dec 1 st 3 sts in from edge every other row 10 more times.

LEFT SLEEVE

Work as for right sleeve, reversing shaping.

BELT

Using smaller needles and Rocher only, CO 17 sts. Work in k1, p1 ribbing, beginning and ending rows with k2. When work measures 51¼ in / 130 cm, BO.

Finishing

Assemble and seam yoke, then seam sleeves and sides of cardigan. With smaller needles, pick up and knit 174 (182, 190, 194, 202) sts at edge of right front and along shoulder of right sleeve, up to center of back neck. Work 3½ in/9 cm / 28 rows in k2, p2 ribbing and then BO. Pick up and knit in the same manner on the left side of cardigan. Seam edges of bands together at center back neck.

18
Tunic

Worked in seed stitch and stockinette,
using Duvetine.

18. Tunic

ONE SIZE	UNIQUE
	Number of skeins
DUVETINE **Grège**	12
from BERGÈRE de France; CYCA #5 (chunky/craft/rug; 8% polyester, 19% polyamide, 73% acrylic; 77 yd/70 m / 50 g)	
Needles: U.S. size 10½ / 6.5 mm	

Stitches used

SEED STITCH:
Row 1 (RS): K1, p1 across.
Row 2: If Row 1 ended with p1: p1, k1 across. If Row 1 ended with k1: k1, p1 across. Repeat Rows 1-2.

STOCKINETTE:
Row 1 (RS): Knit.
Row 2: Purl.
Repeat Rows 1-2.

Gauge

It's very important to knit a gauge swatch (see "The Indispensable Gauge," page 86).
12 sts and 17 rows in St st = 4 x 4 in / 10 x 10 cm.
Adjust needle size to obtain correct gauge if necessary.

Instructions

BACK

CO 77 sts. Work 2 in/5 cm / 10 rows in seed stitch.
Next row: Work 7 sts seed stitch, 63 sts St st, 7 sts seed stitch.
Continue, working seed stitch over seed stitch and St st over St st.
Shoulder and neck: After 26¼ in/67 cm / 116 rows total, at each side, on every other row, BO 3 sts 7 times and then BO 4 sts once. *At the same time* as sixth shoulder dec, BO the 23 center sts for neck and work each side separately, binding off 2 sts at neck edge once.

FRONT

Begin as for back.
Shoulders and neck: When at same length, shape shoulders and neck as for back, but, *at the same time* as second shoulder dec, BO the 17 center sts for neck and work each side separately. At neck edge, on every other row: BO 2 sts twice and then 1 st once.

COLLAR

CO 67 sts. Work 7¾ in/20 cm / 40 rows in seed stitch; BO all sts and set aside.

Finishing

Seam shoulders.
Pin collar to neck edge and then join. Seam sides of collar and turn down to create a rolled collar 4¾ in / 12 cm high.

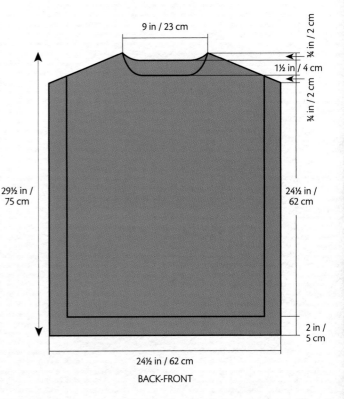

9 in / 23 cm

¾ in / 2 cm

1½ in / 4 cm

¾ in / 2 cm

29½ in / 75 cm

24½ in / 62 cm

2 in / 5 cm

24½ in / 62 cm

BACK-FRONT

19
Crocheted shrug

Worked with double crochet and chain sts, using Coton Fifty.

19. Crocheted shrug

SIZES	S	M	L	XL
	Number of skeins			
COTON FIFTY Zan	5	6	6	7
from BERGÈRE de France; CYCA #1 (sock/fingering/baby; 50% cotton, 50% acrylic; 153 yd/140 m / 50 g)				
Crochet hooks: U.S. sizes C-2 and D-3 / 2.5 and 3 mm				

Stitches used

DOUBLE CROCHET (DC)
= British treble crochet (tr).
Row 1 (RS): Dc in 4th ch from hook, dc across.
Row 2 and all following rows: Ch 3, dc in 2nd dc from end, dc across.

PATTERN STITCH, using larger hook. Worked across a multiple of 16 + 1 sts.
Row 1 (RS): Ch 4, skip 2 sts, * 1 dc, ch 1, skip 1 st *; rep from * to *, ending with 1 dc in 3rd ch of prev row.
Row 2: Ch 4, 1 dc in 2nd dc from end, ch 1, 1 dc, ch 1, * 1 dc in each of next 5 sts, ch 1, (1 dc, ch 1) in each of next 5 sts *; rep from * to *, ending with 1 dc and ch 1 in each of next 2 sts instead of each of next 5 sts and then 1 dc in 2nd ch of prev row.
Rows 3-5: Ch 4, 1 dc in 2nd dc from end, ch 1, * 1 dc in each of next 9 sts, ch 1, (1 dc, ch 1) in each of next 3 sts *; rep from * to *, ending with 1 dc in each of next 9 sts, ch 1, 1 dc in next st, ch 1, 1 dc in 2nd ch of prev row.
Row 6: Work as for Row 2.
Rows 7-9: Ch 4, 1 dc in 2nd dc from end, * ch 1, skip 1 st, 1 dc *; rep from * to *.
Row 10: Ch 3, skip 1st dc, 2 dc, * ch 1, (1 dc, ch 1) in each of next 5 sts, 1 dc in each of next 5 sts *; rep from * to *, ending with 1 dc in each of next 2 sts instead of each of next 5 sts.
Rows 11-13: Ch 3, 1 dc in 2nd dc from end and each of next 3 sts, * ch 1, (1 dc, ch 1) in each of next 3 sts, 1 dc in each of next 9 sts *; rep from * to *, ending with 1 dc in each of next 4 sts instead of each of next 9 sts.
Row 14: Work as for Row 10.
Rows 15-17: Ch 4, 1 dc in 2nd dc from end, * ch 1, skip 1 st, 1 dc *, rep from * to *.
Repeat Rows 2-17.

Gauge

It's very important to crochet a gauge swatch (see "The Indispensable Gauge," page 86).
13 dc + chain "squares" and 12 rows in pattern stitch = 4 x 4 in / 10 x 10 cm.
Adjust hook sizes to obtain correct gauge if necessary.

Instructions

BACK

With smaller hook, ch 99 (107, 119, 127). Work 2 rows in dc [= 97 (105, 117, 125) sts].

Change to larger hook and pattern stitch = 48 (52, 58, 62) dc + chain "squares" in first row of pattern stitch. Begin the second row with (on WS rows, read chart from left to right):

S: Stitch 33 of chart.

M: Stitch 37 of chart.

L: Stitch 43 of chart.

XL: Stitch 47 of chart.

At the same time, from the 3rd row on, inc 1 dc + chain "square" at each side:

S: every other row 3 times.

M: every other row twice, every 3 rows once.

L: every 3 rows twice, every 4 rows once.

XL: every 4 rows 3 times.

To inc 1 dc + chain "square":
- at beg of row: Ch 4, 1 dc in 1st dc of prev row.
- at end of row: In last st, work 1 dc, ch 1, 1 dc.

All increases complete = 54 (58, 64, 68) dc + chain "squares."

Armhole shaping: On the row following the last increase above, ch 3, 2 dc in 1st dc of prev row; complete row, ending with 3 dc in last dc.

Next row: Ch 3, 1 dc in 1st dc of prev row, 2 dc in next st, 1 dc in next st; complete row, ending with 2 dc in each of last 2 sts.

Next row: Ch 3, 1 dc in 1st dc of prev row, 2 dc in next st, 1 dc in each of next 3 sts; work across in pattern stitch until 5 sts rem and then work 1 dc in each of next 3 sts and then 2 dc in each of last 2 sts.

Repeat these increases 4 more times, every time working 2 more dc on either side of pattern stitch section.

Continue, working 15 dc on either side of pattern stitch section, and, *at the same time*, on first row after increases are complete and every 12 rows twice, inc 1 dc + chain "square" 14 sts away from edge [= 14 dc, (1 dc, ch 1, 1 dc)] in next st, work across until 15 sts remain, [(1 dc, ch 1, 1 dc) in next st, 14 dc)].

All increases complete = 15 dc, 58 (62, 68, 72) dc + chain "squares", 15 dc.

Shoulders: After 12½ (13½, 14½, 15¾) in/32 (34, 37, 40) cm / 41 (43, 47, 51) rows total, on every row, at each side, leave unworked:

S: 7 sts twice, 4 dc + chain "squares" twice, 5 dc + chain "squares" once.

M: 7 sts twice, 4 dc + chain "squares" once, 5 dc + chain "squares" twice.

L: 7 sts twice, 5 dc + chain "squares" twice, 6 dc + chain "squares" once.

XL: 7 sts twice, 5 dc + chain "squares" once, 6 dc + chain "squares" twice.

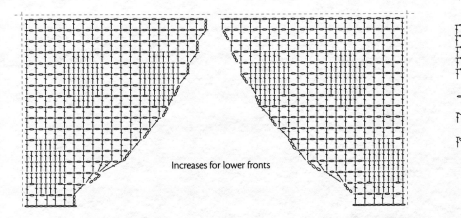

Increases for lower fronts

NECK DECREASES

⌐ ch 1   ⊤ 1 dc

⋏   ⟋⊤ dec 4 sts

⋏   ⋏ dec 2 sts

Next row: Leave the 32 (34, 36, 38) dc + chain "squares" rem unworked for the neck.

RIGHT FRONT

With larger hook, ch 18 (22, 28, 32). Work in pattern stitch = 7 (9, 12, 14) dc + chain "squares" in first row. Beg Row 2 as for back; inc and work armhole edge at left side as for back.

At the same time, from Row 2 onward, at right side, inc 14 dc + chain "squares" over 15 rows, following diagram.

Neck shaping: After 8¾ (9½, 10½, 11¾) in/22 (24, 27, 30) cm / 29 (31, 35, 39) rows total, at right side (see diagram), leave unworked:

S: every row, 4 sts once, 2 sts once, 4 sts once, 2 sts once, 4 sts once, 2 sts 5 times

M: every row, 4 sts once, 2 sts once, 4 sts once, 2 sts once, 4 sts once, 2 sts 6 times

L: every row, 4 sts once, 2 sts once, 4 sts once, 2 sts once, 4 sts once, 2 sts 7 times

XL: every row * 4 sts once, 2 sts once *, rep * to * 3 times, 4 sts once, 2 sts 5 times

Shoulder: After 11¾ (12¾, 13¾, 15) in/30 (32, 35, 38) cm / 39 (41, 45, 49) rows total, at left side, leave sts unworked as for back.

LEFT FRONT

Work as for right front, reversing shaping.

Finishing

Seam shoulders.

Front edges up to back neck: With smaller hook, work 2 rows of dc:

Row 1: Work 1 dc in each chain st at bottom edge of right front, 4 dc in edge of 1st row of right front (= corner), 2 dc in each of following rows up to neck, 5 dc in edge of 1st row of neck (= corner), and then in edge of neck decreases: 2 dc where 2 dc were decreased, 4 dc where 4 dc were decreased, 1 dc in each st of edge of back neck, and then reverse as you move forward toward edge of left front.

Row 2: Work 1 dc in each st of Row 1 *except* over corners of neck. At corners, work 2 dc over center 3 dc of corner.

At end of Row 2, cut yarn and pull through. Seam sides of shrug.

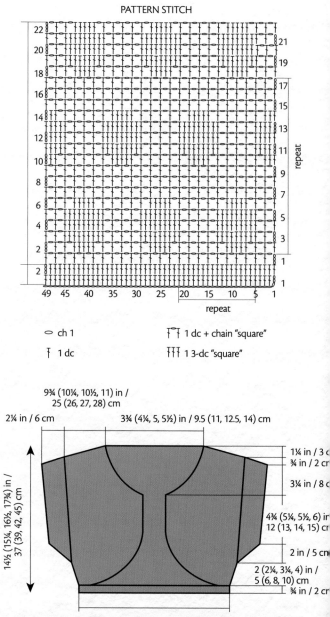

PATTERN STITCH

⬯ ch 1

† 1 dc

†⁻† 1 dc + chain "square"

††† 1 3-dc "square"

9¾ (10¼, 10½, 11) in / 25 (26, 27, 28) cm

2¼ in / 6 cm

3¾ (4¼, 5, 5½) in / 9.5 (11, 12.5, 14) cm

14½ (15¼, 16½, 17¾) in / 37 (39, 42, 45) cm

1¼ in / 3 cm
¾ in / 2 cm
3¼ in / 8 cm
4¾ (5¼, 5½, 6) in / 12 (13, 14, 15) cm
2 in / 5 cm
2 (2¼, 3¼, 4) in / 5 (6, 8, 10) cm
¾ in / 2 cm

14¼ (15¾, 17¼, 18¾) in / 36 (40, 44, 48) cm

BACK-FRONTS

20
Jacket with square collar

Worked in pattern stitch and k2, p2 ribbing, using Bergereine.

20. Jacket with square collar

SIZES	S	M	L	XL
	Number of skeins			
BERGEREINE Pyramide	15	17	18	20
from BERGÈRE de France; CYCA #3 (DK/light worsted; 50% cotton, 50% wool; 104 yd/95 m / 50 g)				
Needles: U.S.sizes 4 and 6 / 3.5 and 4 mm Notions: 4 taupe (or color to match yarn) buttons, 1 in / 23 mm in diameter				

Stitches used

K2, P2 RIBBING, using smaller needles.

PATTERN STITCH, using larger needles. Worked across a multiple of 10 + 6 sts.
Row 1 (RS): K2, p2, k1, * p6, k1, p2, k1 *; rep from * to *, and end with k2 instead of k1.
Row 2: Knit the knits and purl the purls.
Row 3: K2, p2, k1, * p1, p2tog, yo, p2tog, p1, k1, p2, k1 *; rep from * to *, and end with k2 instead of k1.
Row 4 and all following even-numbered rows: Knit the knits and purl the purls; work into each yarnover twice, purling once and knitting once.
Repeat Rows 3-4.

K1, P1 RIBBING, using smaller needles.

Gauge

It's very important to knit a gauge swatch (see "The Indispensable Gauge," page 86).
23 sts and 28 rows in pattern stitch = 4 x 4 in / 10 x 10 cm.
Adjust needle sizes to obtain correct gauge if necessary.

Instructions

BACK

With smaller needles, CO 104 (114, 124, 134) sts. Work 3½ in/9 cm / 30 rows in k2, p2 ribbing, beginning with:
S: P3,
M: K2,
L: K3,
XL: P2,
and, on Row 30, increase 1 st on *each* side = 106 (116, 126, 136) sts. Change to larger needles and pattern stitch, beginning with:
S and L: Stitch 6 of chart.
M and XL: Stitch 1 of chart.
Work in pattern until piece measures 18 (18½, 18½, 18¾) in/46 (47, 47, 48) cm / 134 (136, 136, 140) rows total.
Armhole shaping: At *each* side, on every other row:
S: BO 3 sts once, 2 sts twice, and then 1 st 5 times = 82 sts rem.
M: BO 3 sts once, 2 sts twice, and then 1 st 6 times = 90 sts rem.
L: BO 3 sts once, 2 sts 3 times, and then 1 st 6 times = 96 sts rem.
XL: BO 3 sts twice, 2 sts 3 times, and then 1 st 6 times = 100 sts rem.

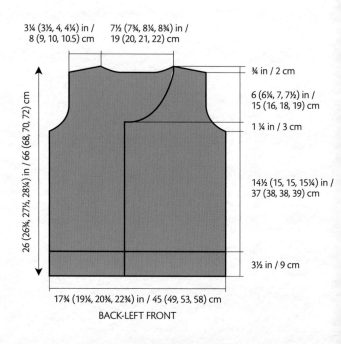

3¼ (3½, 4, 4¼) in / 8 (9, 10, 10.5) cm

7½ (7¾, 8¼, 8¾) in / 19 (20, 21, 22) cm

¾ in / 2 cm

6 (6¼, 7, 7½) in / 15 (16, 18, 19) cm

1 ¼ in / 3 cm

14½ (15, 15, 15¼) in / 37 (38, 38, 39) cm

3½ in / 9 cm

26 (26¾, 27½, 28¼) in / 66 (68, 70, 72) cm

17¾ (19¼, 20¾, 22¾) in / 45 (49, 53, 58) cm

BACK-LEFT FRONT

Continue, working in pattern until piece measures 7 (7½, 8¼, 8¾) in/18 (19, 21, 22) cm from beg of armhole shaping / for 184 (190, 194, 202) rows total.

Shoulders and neck: *At the same time* as first shoulder dec, BO the 32 (34, 36, 38) center sts for neck, and work each side separately. At neck edge, on every other row: BO 3 sts once and then 2 sts once. At the same time, shape shoulder: on every other row,

S: BO 5 sts 4 times.

M: BO 5 sts once, 6 sts 3 times.

L: BO 6 sts 3 times, 7 sts once.

XL: BO 6 sts twice, 7 sts twice.

LEFT FRONT

With smaller needles, CO 59 (64, 69, 74) sts. Work 3½ in/9 cm / 30 rows in k2, p2 ribbing, beginning as for back and increasing 1 st at right side on Row 30 = 60 (65, 70, 75) sts.

Change to larger needles and pattern stitch, beginning as for back.

Armhole shaping: When at same length, shape armhole as for back.

Neck shaping: *At the same time*, when 1¼ in/3 cm from beg of armhole / after 142 (144, 144, 148) rows total, at left side:

S: BO, on every other row, 11 sts once, 3 sts once, 2 sts twice, 1 st 3 times; and then every 4 rows, 1 st 7 times.

M: BO, on every other row, 12 sts once, 3 sts once, 2 sts twice, 1 st once; and then every 4 rows, 1 st 9 times.

L: BO, on every other row, 12 sts once, 3 sts once, 2 sts twice, 1 st once; and then every 4 rows 1 st 10 times.

XL: BO, on every other row, 13 sts once, 3 sts once, 2 sts once, 1 st twice; and then every 4 rows 1 st 11 times.

Shoulder: When at same length, shape shoulder as for back.

RIGHT FRONT

With smaller needles, CO 59 (64, 69, 74) sts. Work 3½ in/9 cm / 30 rows in k2, p2 ribbing, beginning with p2 for all sizes, and increasing 1 st at left on Row 30 = 60 (65, 70, 75) sts.

Change to larger needles and pattern stitch, beginning with Row 1 of pattern.

Armhole shaping: When at same length, shape as for back.

Neck shaping: When at same length, shape on right side as for left front.

Shoulder: When at same length, shape at left side as for back.

SLEEVES

With smaller needles, CO 50 (52, 54, 56) sts. Work 3½ in/9 cm / 30 rows in k2, p2 ribbing, beginning with:

S: K2.

M: K3.

L: P2.

XL: P3.

Change to larger needles. Next row:

S: P3, k1, p2, k1, * p4, k1, p2, k1 *; rep from * to * and end with p3.

M: * P4, k1, p2, k1 *; rep from * to * and end with p4.

L: K1, * p4, k1, p2, k1 *; rep from * to * and end with p4, k1.

XL: P1, k1, * p4, k1, p2, k1 *; rep from * to * and end with p4, k1, p1.

Next row: Knit the knits and purl the purls.

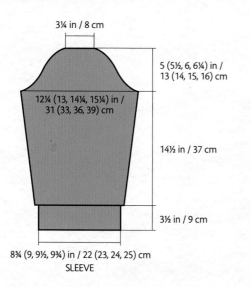

3¼ in / 8 cm

5 (5½, 6, 6¼) in / 13 (14, 15, 16) cm

12¼ (13, 14¼, 15¼) in / 31 (33, 36, 39) cm

14½ in / 37 cm

3½ in / 9 cm

8¾ (9, 9½, 9¾) in / 22 (23, 24, 25) cm

SLEEVE

Next row:

S: P1, * yo, p2, k1, p2, k1, p2 *; rep from * to * and end with yo, p1.

M: P2, * yo, p2, k1, p2, k1, p2 *; rep from * to * and end with yo, p2.

L: K1, p2, * yo, p2, k1, p2, k1, p2 *; rep from * to * and end with yo, p2, k1.

XL: P1, k1, p2, * yo, p2, k1, p2, k1, p2 *; rep from * to * and end with yo, p2, k1, p1.

Next row: Knit the knits and purl the purls; work into each yarnover twice, purling once and knitting once = 64 (66, 68, 70) sts.

Continue working in pattern stitch, beginning on Row 3 of chart with:

S: Stitch 7.

M: Stitch 6.

L: Stitch 5.

XL: Stitch 4.

At the same time, increase on each side:

S: 1 st every 16 rows 5 times = 74 sts.

M: 1 st every 14 rows 6 times = 78 sts.

L: 1 st every 10 rows 9 times = 86 sts.

XL: 1 st every 8 rows 11 times = 92 sts.

Continue in pattern until sleeve measures 18¼ in/46 cm / 134 rows total.

Now shape sleeve cap: on each side every other row,

S: BO 3 sts once, 2 sts twice, 1 st 11 times, 2 sts 3 times, 3 sts once, and then all 20 rem sts.

M: BO 3 sts once, 2 sts twice, 1 st 13 times, 2 sts 3 times, 3 sts once, and then all 20 rem sts.

L: BO 3 sts twice, 2 sts once, 1 st 13 times, 2 sts 3 times, 3 sts twice, and then all 20 rem sts.

XL: BO 3 sts twice, 2 sts twice, 1 st 14 times, 2 sts 3 times, 3 sts twice, and then all 20 rem sts.

COLLAR AND FRONT BANDS

With smaller needles, CO 220 (228, 240, 248) sts. Work 13 sts k1, p1 ribbing, beg with k2 (= left front edge); 194 (202, 214, 222) sts k2, p2 ribbing; and 13 sts k1, p1 ribbing, beg with p1 and ending with k2 (= right front edge).

After 7¾ in/20 cm / 68 rows, place the 207 (215, 227, 235) leftmost sts on a holder, and continue working left front band over the first 13 sts, increasing 1 st at left on first of these rows = 14 sts k1, p1 ribbing.

Work 152 (156, 156, 160) rows and then BO these 14 sts.

Go back to the last 13 sts of the section you set aside (the right front band), and begin working these sts the same way, increasing 1 st at right side on first of these rows = 14 sts k1, p1 ribbing.

Work 19¼ (19¾, 19¾, 20) in/49 (50, 50, 51) cm / 152 (156, 156, 160) rows total and then BO these 14 sts.

Finishing

Join shoulders.

Match center collar stitches with neck and join. Sew front bands to front edges.

Sew sleeves to armholes and then seam sleeves and sides of jacket.

On right front band, make 4 buttonholes 7 sts in from outer edge; place first buttonhole 3¼ in / 8 cm from lower edge, last buttonhole 1¼ in / 3 cm from neck, and then space the other 2 evenly between. Sew on buttons opposite buttonholes.

PATTERN STITCH

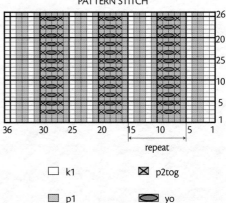

repeat

☐ k1 ⊠ p2tog

▨ p1 ⬭ yo

Tips

The indispensable gauge

Before beginning a pattern, always knit a gauge swatch! This stage is necessary in order for you to know whether the recommended needle size makes sense given your knitting style.

The gauge is the number of stitches and rows you should need to knit to end up with a square that's 4 x 4 in / 10 x 10 cm.

All other stitch and row numbers given in any design are calculated based on the gauge. If your gauge swatch is larger or smaller than the gauge given at the beginning of the pattern, you'll need to switch to a smaller or larger needle size respectively if you want the sizing to come out right.

HOW TO DO IT

Work in the stitch specified and make a square at least 6 x 6 in / 15 x 15 cm with the recommended needle size.

If the material is suitable for steam pressing, steam press your gauge swatch lightly. Stretch your gauge swatch out a little if it's worked with ribbing.

With a ruler, measure out 4 x 4 in / 10 x 10 cm in the center of your 6 x 6 in / 15 x 15 cm square and count the number of stitches and rows.

Compare your result with the gauge given in the pattern.

IF YOUR SWATCH HAS MORE STITCHES AND ROWS THAN THE GAUGE GIVEN

You knit a little bit tightly; knit a new gauge swatch with larger needles, and you should be able to match the gauge (or at least get closer).

IF YOUR SWATCH HAS FEWER STITCHES AND ROWS THAN THE GAUGE GIVEN

You knit a little bit loosely; knit a new gauge swatch with smaller needles, and you should be able to match the gauge (or at least get closer).

NOTE!

It's important that you get the number of stitches specified in the gauge, at the very least, since that's the basis for the pattern's design and proportions. You can adjust the number of rows as you work to obtain the correct measurements much more easily than the number of stitches per row.

Some definitions

ABBREVIATIONS

beg	begin(s)/beginning
BO	bind off (= British cast off)
cm	centimeters
CO	cast on
dec	decrease
in	inch(es)
inc	increase
k	knit
k2tog	knit 2 together = 1 st decreased, right-leaning
k3tog	knit 3 together= 2 sts decreased, right-leaning
mm	millimeters
p	purl
pm	place marker
prev	previous
psso	pass slipped stitch over
rem	remain(s)(ing)
rep	repeat
RS	right side
sl	slip
st(s)	stitch(es)
St st	stockinette stitch (= British stocking stitch)
WS	wrong side
yo	yarnover

Pattern stitches

Instructions for these stitches are written out *and* charted; on the chart, each box represents one stitch on one row. Charts are accompanied by chart keys that explain what each symbol or color means. The chart always shows the right side of work. However, even with a chart, it's not always easy to figure out exactly how to work a stitch. Even if you prefer reading charts to written instructions, it's a good idea to read through the instructions before starting.

"Work the stitches as they appear" means you should knit the knits and purl the purls as those stitches face you.

Seaming with running stitch

Align edges to be seamed with RS facing RS.
Start with the needle at the back; pierce both layers of knitting and draw through to front, and then pierce again about 2 rows of knitting further on and draw through to back.

Moss stitch

Cast on an odd number of stitches.
Row 1: (K1, p1) across, ending the row with k1.
Row 2: (P1, k1) across, ending the row with p1.
Row 3: (P1, k1) across, ending the row with p1.
Row 4: (K1, p1) across, ending the row with k1.
Repeat Rows 1-4.

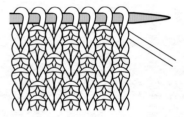

Invisible seams

Thread a yarn needle or tapestry needle with the same color as the work.

Work on the RS. In the pieces you're joining, direct your needle and yarn/thread around the horizontal part of the first and second stitches and then draw together tightly enough that the edges are flush and the seam hardly shows. If the edges are a little uneven, begin with the horizontal parts of the second and third stitches instead.

Tips

Chain stitch (ch)

Foundation stitch for crochet. Make a loop; insert the crochet hook through it. Wrap the yarn around the hook and pull the hook back out of the loop with the yarn still around it. Now the hook is already through a loop, made by the yarn that was pulled through the first loop—wrap the yarn around the hook again and pull the hook back out of this second loop. Continue until you have the number of chain stitches specified.

Double crochet (dc; = British treble/tr)

With the hook already in a loop, wrap the yarn around the hook. Push the hook through the two upper loops of the stitch on the previous row, wrap the yarn around the hook again, and pull the hook back through the stitch on the previous row. There are now three loops on the hook. Wrap the yarn around the hook and pull it through two loops, leaving two loops on the hook. Wrap the yarn around the hook again and pull it through those two loops, leaving one loop on the hook. One double crochet stitch is complete.

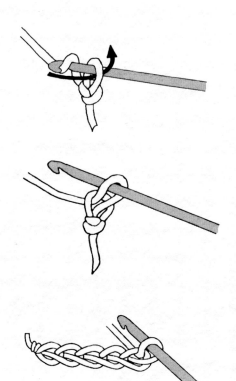

Other notes

When working with a new skein of yarn, it's often best to pull from the center of the skein instead of the outside. This way, the skein won't roll around and the yarn will tangle less. You can also wind your skeins into balls and pull the yarn from the center of the ball for easier knitting. Either way, you'll be able to knit much more quickly.

The best way to get your knitting even and regular is to practice: knit small squares, doll clothing, accessories ... Practice until the motions of knitting are easy and natural, and then start trying out mittens and scarves, and so on. Feel free to choose pattern yarns that are multicolored or mottled to help hide irregularities and minor mistakes.

Always complete the row before you set down your knitting, or the stitches might stretch out and become misshapen. It's not a bad idea to count and re-count your stitches regularly, in case you've accidentally slipped one or picked one up—the more often you count, the sooner you'll notice any problems, and the less work you'll have to rip out if you find a problem.

To keep your edges nice, always work the first edge stitch with a little more tension; edge stitches tend to get a little loose over time compared to the rest of the row. (On a sweater or cardigan, these edge stitches are often hidden by the seams during finishing.)

When starting a new skein, always do so at the beginning of a row. At the end of the last row, leaving about 4 in / 10 cm, cut the yarn from the old skein. Begin the next row with the new skein. The two tails this creates can be woven into the edges, which means you won't end up with an unsightly knot sticking out of the middle of a row. Leftover lengths of yarn can be used for joining and seaming.

To pick up a dropped stitch, it may help to have a crochet hook. Working in stockinette, knit until the point where the stitch was dropped. Slide the crochet hook into the dropped stitch and use the hook to catch the horizontal strand just below. Pull that strand through the dropped stitch. Do this as many times as needed to reach the row you're currently working, and then move the stitch from the crochet hook to the left needle and knit normally.

If you plan to knit with multiple yarns held together, it may be a good idea to make a new ball of yarn for yourself by winding one from the skeins you're planning to use held together. This way, when you knit from your multi-yarn ball, the tension on each strand of yarn will always be the same, your yarns won't get tangled with each other, and different colors or textures of yarn should be visible throughout.

To avoid accidental color variations, never start a project with leftover yarn if you don't have enough to complete it. Even yarn of the same color from the same company may not be from the same dyelot. If it's less than three months since you purchased the yarn, you may be able to return any intact skeins and then buy a new selection that is all from the same dyelot—ask your local yarn store or check an online store's policy.

If your acrylic yarns have a tendency toward pilling, don't pull the yarn pills off the surface of your garment; use scissors or a precision knife to cut them away instead.

Acknowledgments

A big "thank you" to Cléa

Cléa lives between Nancy, France—where she is a student—and Paris, where she has been working as a plus-size model for over four years. She loves music, singing, and going to the movies, and has an equal passion for fashion and for anything that can flatter a few curves! Modeling these designs, so pretty and so straightforward to make, has tempted her to take up knitting, too.

T-shirt: Boden. Pants: 3 Suisses. Belt: H&M. Shoes: 3 Suisses.

Jeans: Woman Curves. Bra: 3 Suisses. Necklace: Boden. Shoes: 3 Suisses.

Undershirt: Woman Curves. Skirt: Pauline et Julie. Hat and belt: 3 Suisses.

Pants: Courbes&Co. Necklace: owned by model. Clutch: 3 Suisses.

Tank top and pants: Marina Rinaldi. Necklace: owned by model. Shoes: 3 Suisses.

Dress: Boden. Bracelet: owned by model.

Shirt and jeans: Woman Curves. Shoes: 3 Suisses.

Pantsuit: Woman Curves. Clutch: owned by model. Shoes: 3 Suisses.

Shirt: Pauline et Julie. Leggings: Boden. Shoes: 3 Suisses.

Acknowledgments
A big "thank you" to Raphaëlle

An artist in every sense of the word, Raphaëlle Dess is an author, composer, performer, actress, and musician. Her face might look familiar—she has sung and done stage work over several years (including performing in operas and musicals).

Radiant, sensitive, and energetic all at once, Raphaëlle is also a handcrafter: She began knitting at the age of seven, a family tradition that was passed down to her by her mother.

Dress: H&M. Necklace: Emma&Chloé. Clutch: owned by model.

Blouse, skirt, and belt: Onoz.

Tank top and pants: Marina Rinaldi. Shoes: 3 Suisses.

Blouse: Boden. Pants: Marina Rinaldi.
Shoes: Boden.

T-shirt: Boden. Jeans: Marina Rinaldi.
Hat: Woman Curves.

Shirt: 3 Suisses. Pants: Marina Rinaldi.

Shirt: Woman Curves. Jeans: 3 Suisses. Hat and
belt: Woman Curves. Shoes: 3 Suisses.

Shirt: 3 Suisses. Jeans: Woman Curves. Earrings:
owned by model. Purse: 3 Suisses.

Shirt: Boden. Pants: Marina Rinaldi.
Shoes: 3 Suisses.

Yarn Suppliers

Bergère de France (North America)
100 Marie-Victorin Blvd
Boucherville QC
J4B 1V6
Canada
www.bergeredefrance.com

LoveKnitting.com
www.loveknitting.com/us

If you are unable to obtain any of the yarn used in this book, it can be replaced with a yarn of a similar weight and composition. Please note, however, the finished projects may vary slightly from those shown, depending on the yarn used. Try www.yarnsub.com for suggestions.

For more information on selecting or substituting yarn, contact your local yarn shop or an online store; they are familiar with all types of yarns and would be happy to help you. Additionally, the online knitting community at Ravelry.com has forums where you can post questions about specific yarns. Yarns come and go so quickly these days and there are so many beautiful yarns available.